Becoming a Culture Architect

Roseanne Lazarus de Romero

DEDICATION

This book is dedicated to the many companies and diverse opportunities I experienced over the span of my career. The leaders (both good and not-so-good) who showed me the impact and importance of creating a culture that fuels employee engagement and motivation. It's for the brilliant and supportive colleagues I've had the honor to work with over the years. It's for my family, who inspired me and knew I could do this, even when I doubted myself.

CONTENTS

1
INTRODUCTION: WHY CULTURE DOESN'T HAPPEN BY ACCIDENT

If there's one lesson my career has taught me, it's that culture never stands still, it will evolve on its own, but not always in ways that support success. Every organization I've been part of, whether thriving or struggling, had a culture. The difference was whether it was intentional or accidental.

If you've ever walked into a workplace where people are guarded, disengaged, or just "going through the motions," you know what happens when culture is left to chance. It drifts. And it often drifts in the wrong direction. It calcifies, hardens, and secures itself making it difficult to change.

Now contrast that with the companies you've seen or worked with, ones that feel alive. People are energized, decisions get made faster, and the business can adapt to challenges because there's trust in the system. That's not an accident. That's design.

Let me share a couple of personal examples.

> In the late '90s, technical talent was in constant motion. Employees often jumped ship for higher salaries, bonuses, or perks, and our company's attrition rate around 18–20% reflected that reality. Because we were bound by federal contract salary limits, we couldn't always compete on pay. I was hired specifically to find a way to retain top talent for this company.

> When I entered the company, based on the turnover rate, I expected to find dissatisfaction in the overall engagement of its employees. Yet from my first day, I sensed something different. This company with a 40+ year history had a culture that was warm, authentic, and human, palpable from the receptionist to the CEO who personally welcomed me. People laughed, supported one another, and truly cared. It was a workplace full of heart. I don't remember seeing a single value hanging on the wall or presented on the company website. Yet, I felt those values through consistent and pervasive behaviors, ones that had been passed down and kept alive across four decades.

Instead of rushing to solutions, I dug into exit surveys and spoke with employees. The pattern was clear: people left for money, but they stayed for belonging, mission, and meaningful relationships. Culture was the differentiator.

One small initiative brought this to life: we launched an alumni newsletter to keep in touch with former employees. To our surprise, about 15% reached out to explore returning. The grass wasn't greener after all. Culture really did matter more than money.

On the contrary, I also remember working with a different company with a completely different example of culture.

Although the organization was still young, its culture already felt fragmented: rigid in some areas, half-formed in others, and often contradictory.

I interviewed for a position as a Talent Development Leader. I was attracted to the company and the role by the clarity in the job description and the culture represented on the company's career website highlighting its values.

The hiring process was my first clue that something was off. What should have been straightforward stretched over months, with long silences, redundant interviews, and a panel that felt more like an interrogation than a dialogue. By the time I met the CHRO weeks later, I'd already ignored several warning signs.

Onboarding only reinforced the disconnect. There was no excitement, no personal touch; just forms, information overload, and a sense I was on my own. It took a full week before my manager found time to meet with me.

Ironically, I had been hired to drive cultural change. But what I found was not one culture, but many. Each leader operated differently. The company declared "Our People Matter" and "We Empower Employees," yet my experience, influenced by delayed decisions, lack of connection, and a process devoid of care, contradicted those very values.

What I learned repeatedly throughout my career was that culture will create itself if not intentionally guided. Companies craft vision and mission statements and select their chosen values which often become wall decorations instead of true shared behaviors.

For years, employee engagement has been a cornerstone of organizational health assessments. Companies invest heavily in tools like annual surveys, pulse checks, and feedback platforms. The idea is simple: measure engagement, identify problem areas, and intervene accordingly.

But there's a fundamental flaw in this approach – it's reactive by nature. Engagement surveys typically capture how employees feel after decisions, structures, and culture have already shaped their day-to-day experience. This creates a lag between cause and effect, making it harder to address issues before they escalate.

What many leaders overlook is that engagement is not a standalone goal. It's the natural outcome of a strong, intentional culture. Rather than waiting to measure employee dissatisfaction or disconnection, forward-thinking organizations are shifting their focus toward proactively designing the culture they want. This approach moves beyond treating engagement as a diagnostic tool and positions culture as a strategic asset.

Culture Doesn't Belong to HR Alone

One of the most common misconceptions I hear is that culture is "an HR thing." As a matter of fact, every position I occupied across 9 companies and 7 industries was aligned to the HR department. Just do a quick job search on LinkedIn for Talent and Culture jobs. You'll see that most report to HR. Don't get me wrong, HR plays a critical role in carrying culture through systems, policies, and people practices. But the truth is, **culture is a leadership thing.**

At its heart, culture is the shared system of meaning: the beliefs, behaviors, and unspoken rules that guide how work really gets done. And shaping that system belongs to those leading the business.

That's where the role of the **Culture Architect** comes in. A culture architect doesn't just inherit culture; they intentionally design it. They understand that culture is not fluff, not the "soft side," but one of the most powerful levers of strategy and performance.

In the role I described earlier, hired to build the company's talent development function, I quickly realized two things: I couldn't do it alone, and culture should never sit solely on HR's shoulders. When HR is positioned as the "guardian of culture," the team ends up reacting and enforcing rather than leading as innovators, catalysts, strategists, or what I call architects.

Culture must be designed collectively by the leadership team and owned by the entire organization. That means redefining the role: bringing leaders together to co-author the culture, securing their commitment to it, and ensuring it is lived consistently through behaviors, processes, systems, and rituals.

The Journey Ahead

This book is about becoming that kind of architect who builds culture with the same rigor and imagination as a blueprint for a building.

We'll go on a three-part journey:

> **The Case for Culture by Design** — why culture is the silent partner of strategy, and why leaders ignore it at their peril.
>
> **The Blueprint of Culture** — the building blocks of a strong, vibrant culture, from purpose and values to rituals and practices.
>
> **Becoming a Culture Architect** — how to assess, design, implement, and sustain culture intentionally, even in times of disruption.

This won't just be theory. Along the way, I'll share real examples, practical tools, and reflection questions you can apply right away in your own culture by design journey.

A Call to Curiosity

Here's what I want you to keep in mind as you read: **culture isn't optional.** You already have one. The real question is whether it's the culture you want, or the one you've settled into by default.

The future belongs to culture architects: the leaders who are bold enough to design, nurture, and evolve culture as a living advantage.

My hope is that by the end of this book, you'll not only see the urgency of culture by design, but you'll also have the mindset, tools, and confidence to begin shaping a culture that fuels both performance and people.

2
THE CASE FOR CULTURE BY DESIGN:
CULTURE = STRATEGY'S SILENT PARTNER

Every leader I've worked with has a strategy. Growth plans. Market expansions. New products. Efficiency initiatives. Strategy is where executives tend to put their time and energy because strategy feels tangible. You can chart it on a slide deck, map milestones, track KPIs.

But here's the truth I've seen play out time and again: **culture quietly makes or breaks strategy.**

When culture and strategy align, magic happens. People move with purpose, decisions stick, and energy becomes contagious. Strategy turns into action because everyone understands *why* they're doing what they're doing. People feel motivated to execute it. Obstacles are met with creativity and resilience.

But when culture and strategy are at odds, execution stalls. Initiatives drag on, good ideas die in meeting rooms, and leaders scratch their heads wondering why their carefully crafted plans aren't implemented. I often hear it said that: *culture eats strategy for breakfast...* but I'd add: *for lunch, and dinner too.*

> I once consulted with a company that acquired another to expand its market presence. On paper, the deal looked perfect: the financials lined up, and the strategic fit was undeniable. But there was one fatal oversight: no one thought about culture.
>
> Employees of the acquired company never truly joined the new organization. They kept wearing t-shirts with the old logo, swapped stories about "how things used to be," and quietly resisted aligning with their new employer. Their loyalty remained with a company that technically no longer existed.
>
> This isn't unusual. This kind of oversight is more common than people think. Up to 60% of M&A failures can be attributed to cultural misalignment, not a glitch in the spreadsheets, but a failure to bring hearts and minds on board. Without intentional cultural

integration, most mergers and acquisitions stumble. Engagement slips. Talent disengages. And in this case, the organization was eventually acquired itself and disappeared.

Culture is emotional. It lives in people's sense of identity and belonging. And no matter how brilliant the strategy or financial logic is, without culture as the driver, strategy alone will not succeed.

The Hidden Costs of Neglecting Culture

Neglecting culture isn't neutral, it's expensive. Research consistently links poor culture to higher turnover, disengagement, and stalled innovation.

Here are a few statistics that research has shown:

- **Engagement boosts performance**: Gallup reports that highly engaged teams drive 21% greater profitability with 59% less turnover compared to disengaged ones.
- **Innovation and retention**: Deloitte research shows companies with strong cultures outperform competitors by up to 200% and enjoy 30% higher innovation and 40% better employee retention.
- **Meanings beyond stats**: Strong cultures deliver 10% higher customer ratings and 20% more sales, while poor culture costs the global economy $8.8 trillion in lost performance.

I've watched leaders spend millions chasing efficiency or market share without realizing the real drag was cultural. Strategy got the investment, but culture was the silent tax.

Culture by the Numbers

- **21% greater profitability, 59% lower turnover** — Gallup
- **200% performance boost, 30% more innovation** — Deloitte
- **10% higher customer ratings, 20% increase in sales** — Enculture
- **$8.8 trillion lost due to low engagement** — Deloitte

The best business strategy will fail without an aligned culture to drive it. Yet, most companies put less time and intention into culture creation than strategic planning. Culture is not just a byproduct of strategy. It is a critical enabler that shapes, drives, and sustains strategic success.

Culture will develop, if not intentionally, then accidental, and usually in the wrong direction. There is a direct cause and effect relationship between culture and business outcomes.

Productivity and Performance: A clear, aligned culture gives people focus and clarity. They know what "great" looks like. Teams that trust each other, feel safe to speak up and are aligned on values perform better – period.

Why it matters: Psychological safety (a cultural trait) is the #1 predictor of high performing teams (Google's Project Aristotle).

Innovation and Adaptability: Cultures that celebrate experimentation and learning create more breakthroughs. Fear-based or blame heavy cultures kill creativity and slow down change.

Why it matters: In a fast-moving world, the companies that adapt fastest win – and that requires a culture where people feel safe to try, fail, and learn.

Employee Engagement and Retention: Strong culture = people who are more motivated, loyal, and energized. Companies with high engagement see up to 21% higher profitability and 59% less turnover

(Gallup)

> Why it matters: Replacing an employee can cost 1.5-2 times their salary. Culture keeps people from walking out the door.

Reputation and Talent Attraction: Culture is a brand in the talent market. People talk – Glassdoor, LinkedIn, word-of-mouth. Companies known for great culture attract top talent even in tight markets.

> Why it matters: The best candidates have options. Culture is often the deciding factor.

Customer Experience: Happy, aligned employees create happy, loyal customers. Your internal culture shows up in how your people treat customers.

> Why it matters: Companies with strong cultures see higher customer satisfaction, loyalty, and Net Promoter Scores (NPS).

Culture has a huge impact on business outcomes, It's one of the biggest levers for performance, retention, innovation, and brand reputation.

Culture isn't "soft stuff". It's a strategic asset. When done well, it directly contributes to growth, resilience, and competitive advantage.

Case Studies: When Culture Accelerates Strategy

When Satya Nadella became CEO of Microsoft in 2014, he took key steps to shift the culture known for its competitive internal culture, siloed teams, and stagnating innovation to one of collaboration, learning, and empathy. He encouraged a growth mindset, led with empathy, redefined the mission statement, modeled vulnerability and humility, broke down silos, aligned culture with strategy, communicated consistently and authentically, and focused on leadership development.

Due to the courageous culture shift, Microsoft saw results in greater innovation (e.g., Azure growth, embracing open source), stock price increased 10X from 2014 to 2024 and Microsoft became a leader in cloud and AI.

Airbnb's culture shift was less about radical change and more about rediscovering its original values through crisis and aligning them more authentically with how it operates and serves. This significant shift occurred during and after the COVID-19 crisis. They reaffirmed their core mission, led with transparency and empathy during crisis, shifted from hyper-growth to grounded focus (let go of expansion to refocus on its core product), flattened hierarchies, embraced trust, remote, and flexible work and modeled a founder-led culture.

What happens when you discover your culture has taken a detour?

Over the many years of my career, I've experienced leaders who acknowledge that their culture is broken or moving in the wrong direction. When I've asked them what they are going to do about it, their responses have been similar:

- "We can't change it! It runs too deep!"
- "We'll be met with resistance. We don't have time or energy to deal with that!"
- "Our engagement survey shows that it's only in a few areas of our company that people are disengaged. We'll leave it up to those leaders/managers to fix."
- "HR will design programs to address what's broken."

Like the above examples of Microsoft and Airbnb, both cultures needed transformations. True cultural transformation demands not just strategy, but bold, sustained courage. Culture shifts often require challenging norms, confronting conflict, or disrupting revenue-driving habits. Culture is personal. Shifting requires emotional and interpersonal bravery.

Acts of courage take different forms. For example, courage is required to acknowledge the need for change. Owning up to problems in your current culture requires raw honesty and a willingness to admit that the *"emperor is wearing no clothes"*. Leaders must role model vulnerability, admitting missteps and committing to learning, to truly solicit accurate and reflective information about culturally-toxic traits.

Another courageous hurdle for leaders is facing internal resistance. There will be naysayers: those who disagree with the need for change and are comfortable with status quo conditions and behaviors. There will be power holders who will see change as a surrendering of status, resisting defensively to protect their positions. And teams who are performing well will be skeptical over the need for change as they prefer to stay sheltered within their cocoon of high performance. Courageous leaders must find ways to overcome these resistors and bring them together into a unified and cohesive effort.

Courage is not just a personal virtue; it's a strategic necessity for cultural evolution. *What part of your culture are you too afraid to change, and what might happen if you found the courage?*

The Bottom Line

Strategy tells you where you want to go. Culture determines whether you'll get there.

And here's the key shift: **culture isn't just a support system for strategy. It's a strategic lever itself.** When leaders embrace culture as a business driver, it becomes an accelerant. When they ignore it, culture becomes the anchor holding everything back.

That's why designing culture intentionally is not optional. It's leadership's most powerful, and most underleveraged, responsibility.

Reflection Questions:

1. When you think about your current organization, what is the "heartbeat" you feel most strongly, and does it align with the values your company claims to hold?

2. Where do you see culture showing up most clearly in daily work: in hiring, meetings, decision-making, or somewhere else?

3. What recent experience (positive or negative) revealed the "real" culture of your organization?

3

PREVENTING CULTURE CRACKS BEFORE THEY BREAK

Most leaders remember the nursery rhyme: "Humpty Dumpty sat on a wall, Humpty Dumpty had a great fall. All the king's horses and all the king's men, couldn't put Humpty together again."

It's a simple children's rhyme, but it also offers a sharp metaphor for workplace culture. Once cracks appear, and once trust and consistency shatter, no amount of patching is enough to restore things exactly as they were. Culture, like Humpty, is fragile. And waiting until the fall makes repair far harder than prevention.

The Silent Cracks That Employees Notice

Culture doesn't usually break all at once. It fractures slowly, in small, almost invisible ways, through the everyday moments employees observe and interpret.

- Promotions vs. Frameworks: A competency model may provide employees with a clear roadmap for development. Yet, they often see inconsistencies: roles with the same titles carrying very different workloads, scopes, and expectations, or employees promoted without demonstrating the criteria that were communicated as essential. When what's written doesn't match what's observed, trust in the system erodes. A crack appears.
- Recognition of Effort vs. Impact: Leaders may talk about balance, but when the late-night emailers and weekend warriors are celebrated, employees see that effort, not outcomes, matters most. Another crack.
- Tolerance of Bad Behavior: When toxic performers are ignored or rewarded, employees assume results excuse disrespect. The crack deepens.

Each moment seems small, but like fractures in an eggshell, once they spread, they're nearly impossible to glue back together.

Leadership Inconsistencies: The Force Behind the Fall

Employees quickly notice when leaders say one thing and do another. These inconsistencies are the weight that eventually pushes Humpty off the wall:

- Preaching balance while rewarding burnout.
- Declaring inclusivity while ignoring bias.
- Prioritizing innovation in words but cutting budgets in practice.

Over time, these cracks weaken trust. And when the culture finally "falls," the break is public and damaging: disengagement, turnover, cynicism, and lost credibility.

The HR Dilemma: Watching the Cracks Spread

HR often sees the cracks first. They hear the whispers, read the survey comments, and notice the misalignments. Yet, too often, they aren't empowered to act, especially when cultural fractures come from the very top.

And here's the reality: HR shouldn't be expected to keep gluing Humpty together. Culture isn't their job to enforce. Culture is the responsibility of leaders who model it every day. If leaders offload accountability to HR, cracks only widen until the fall becomes inevitable.

Why Cracks Are So Hard to Repair

Once employees form their interpretations, they harden into unwritten rules. People learn quickly what really gets rewarded, who really holds power, and which values really apply. And once those beliefs set in, they're resistant to change.

Repair requires more than a new memo or a refreshed set of posters. It takes:

- Leadership awareness: acknowledging the cracks, not ignoring them.
- Courage from the C-suite: to change long-held habits and hold one another accountable.
- Alignment at the top: around purpose, values, vision, behaviors, processes, systems, and even rituals.
- Consistency in execution: so employees see not just words but lived commitment.

This work isn't quick or cosmetic. It requires dedicated time, sustained effort, and the willingness to confront uncomfortable truths.

The Payoff: A Stronger Shell, Not a Fragile One

The good news is that when leaders lean in and repair culture before it collapses, the results are powerful:

- Productivity improves as employees align around shared priorities.
- Engagement rises when people feel connected to a culture they trust.
- Profitability grows as high performance is achieved without the drag of cynicism or disengagement.
- Top talent is both attracted and retained, because people want to work where culture is real and consistent.

The Bottom Line

Every organization has cracks. The question is whether leaders notice them early or wait until the fall.

If culture is left to fracture under the weight of inconsistencies and misaligned behaviors, no amount of repair after the fact will fully restore what's lost. But with leadership courage, clarity, and consistency, culture doesn't have to be fragile like Humpty Dumpty. It can be strong, resilient, and capable of carrying the business to greater success.

So, leaders must ask themselves: Are we guarding against the cracks, or are we waiting for the fall?

Reflection Questions

As you consider the "cracks" that can quietly weaken culture, take a moment to reflect on your own leadership practices:

1. **Where might inconsistencies exist between what I say and what I reward?**
   – Do my recognition practices align with the values I claim to champion?

2. **Am I unintentionally tolerating "cracks" in our culture?**
   – Are there behaviors, attitudes, or exceptions I overlook because results seem to justify them?

3. **How clearly do employees see the connection between advancement and our stated frameworks?**
   – Would they describe our promotions and development paths as transparent and fair?

4. **What signals am I sending about work-life balance?**
   – Do I celebrate outcomes and sustainable practices—or late nights and constant availability?

5. **What role am I modeling as a leader in shaping culture?**
   – Am I leaving culture to HR, or am I personally accountable for the behaviors and consistency my team observes?

6. **If employees were asked to describe the "unwritten rules" of our organization, what would they say?**
   – Do those unwritten rules reflect the culture we want—or cracks we've ignored?

7. **Am I catching the cracks early?**
   – Do I invite feedback regularly enough to see where trust or alignment may be slipping before it spreads?

4
THE SCIENCE AND SOUL/THE HARD AND THE SOFT OF CULTURE

When people ask me to define culture, I often smile because it's one of those things you know when you feel it. You can measure it, analyze it, put it into charts and reports, but you also sense it in your gut. Culture is both data and emotion. It's science and soul.

I've walked into organizations where you could feel the heartbeat of the culture in the very first five minutes: a receptionist who greeted me like a valued guest, colleagues laughing and supporting one another, a CEO who stopped to chat in the hallway. And I've walked into others where the silence in the lobby spoke volumes: guarded stares, hushed tones, and an atmosphere that felt heavy before I even met my first contact. Both experiences told me more about those workplaces than any engagement survey ever could.

Culture has two dimensions. One is measurable, rational, and backed by research. The other is emotional, human, and deeply personal. The healthiest organizations know how to balance both.

The Science of Culture

Researchers have been studying workplace culture for decades, and the findings are remarkably consistent: culture isn't just a "soft" factor. It's a hard driver of business performance.

- Gallup research shows that **highly engaged teams achieve 21% greater profitability** than their peers.

- Harvard Business Review reports that companies with strong performance-enhancing cultures see **4x revenue growth** compared to those with weak cultures.

- Deloitte found that **94% of executives and 88% of employees believe a distinct workplace culture is crucial to business success**.In other words: culture is measurable. It shows up in employee engagement, turnover rates, productivity metrics, leadership trust scores, and even innovation pipelines. You can see it in how hiring decisions are made, how recognition is given, and how conflict is handled.

When leaders try to separate culture from business strategy, they miss the point. Culture *is* strategy's strongest enabler, or its quietest killer.

The Soul of Culture

Yet, culture isn't just about statistics or KPIs. It's about the lived experience of people. It's the stories employees tell each other, the traditions they share, the way they describe their work to family and friends.

I've seen employees wear company T-shirts long after leaving an organization because the experience meant something to them. I've seen teams rally behind one another during a crisis, showing a level of care that no policy manual could ever mandate. These moments are the *soul* of culture.

And make no mistake: culture is emotional. Belonging, trust, and meaning are the glue that keep people engaged. When those are present, employees show up with energy and commitment. When they're absent, disengagement and turnover rise quickly.

Harvard Business Review has highlighted that employees who feel a strong sense of purpose are **2.6 times more likely to stay at their organizations long-term**. That's not just an HR metric — that's the soul of culture at work.

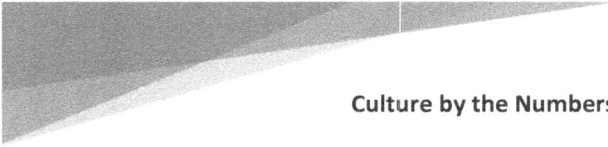

Culture by the Numbers

- **23%**: Profitability boost for highly engaged teams (Gallup)
- **4x**: Revenue growth for strong vs. weak cultures (HBR)
- **94%**: Executives who say culture is key to success (Deloitte)
- **60%**: M&A failures linked to cultural misalignment (Deloitte/Instill)
- **2.6x**: Likelihood of employees staying when they feel a strong sense of purpose (HBR)

The Integration: Science + Soul

The mistake many leaders make is leaning too far in one direction. Some treat culture as purely *science*, measured only in engagement scores, benchmark reports, and KPIs. Others treat it as purely *soul*, all slogans, posters, and inspiring town halls with little follow-through.

But culture thrives when both dimensions are honored. The science gives leaders clarity, focus, and evidence. The soul gives employees connection, meaning, and energy. One without the other is incomplete. Together, they make culture not just a concept, but a lived reality.

Practical Look: How Technology and Process Shape Company Culture

When leaders talk about "culture," it often feels like the soft side of business: values, behaviors, trust, and belonging. On the other hand, technology and processes are considered the hard side—tangible systems, tools, and structures that drive efficiency. Too often, companies treat these as separate domains. But the hard and soft sides constantly influence each other, for better or worse.

Technology and Process as Culture Shapers

Culture isn't just what leaders say or how employees behave. It's reinforced by the systems people work with every day.

- **Technology as a culture amplifier**: The tools we choose can reinforce transparency, collaboration, and inclusion. Or, unintentionally promote silos, control, and exclusion.

- **Process as a cultural signal**: Processes aren't neutral; they signal what the organization truly values. A hiring process designed for speed may emphasize efficiency over fairness. A performance review process that encourages dialogue and development fosters growth; one that focuses solely on numbers reinforces competition.

The HR Lens: The Everyday Hard Side That Shapes the Soft Side

Some of the most influential culture-shaping technologies and processes sit within HR:

- **Payroll & benefits systems** – Employees don't just expect to be paid accurately and on time; the way benefits are communicated and administered shapes whether people feel valued, supported, and secure.

- **Compliance processes** – Policies, reporting mechanisms, and training are more than check-the-box exercises; they demonstrate whether the company truly prioritizes fairness, equity, and safety.

- **Data collection & analysis** – Employee surveys, engagement platforms, and workforce analytics don't just measure culture; they influence it. If leaders act on the insights, trust grows. If data disappears into a black hole, cynicism sets in.

- **Training, development, and LMS** – Learning platforms and training processes signal whether growth is truly a priority. A clunky LMS or mandatory-only training communicates compliance over development. A modern LMS with self-directed learning and career pathways signals investment in people's futures.

- **HR technology platforms** – Recruitment tools, performance management systems, and learning portals frame how employees experience opportunity, growth, and recognition in the company.

In each case, the "hard side" is also a moment of truth for culture—employees experience culture in how smooth, fair, and human these processes feel.

When the Hard Side Interferes with the Soft Side

Problems arise when technology and process are implemented without considering cultural impact:

- Over-automation erodes trust – Tools meant to streamline can leave employees feeling monitored or undervalued.

- Rigid processes undermine agility – Overly complex approval structures or standardized procedures can slow innovation and create frustration.

- Misaligned HR tech creates disengagement – If performance reviews are cumbersome, the LMS is outdated, or payroll errors go unresolved, employees quickly conclude that culture is more rhetoric than reality.

When the Hard Side Strengthens the Soft Side

On the flip side, thoughtful alignment between hard and soft creates powerful culture reinforcement:

- **Technology enabling values** – If a company values transparency, HR dashboards and self-service portals can empower employees to see and manage their own data.

- **Processes supporting inclusion** – Structured recruitment tools can ensure diverse candidates are considered fairly, embedding equity into daily practice.

- **Systems that promote growth** – A well-designed LMS with career pathways, skill-building opportunities, and development resources demonstrates that growth and learning are core to the culture.

- **Everyday systems that build trust** – Seamless payroll, responsive benefits support, and visible follow-through on engagement surveys tell employees: "We care, and we're listening."

Leadership's Role: Bridging Hard and Soft

Leaders need to stop viewing technology and culture as separate investments. Every tool or process change is a cultural intervention. Before rolling out a new HR platform, compliance procedure, or training initiative, leaders should ask:

- How does this align with our values?

- What cultural behaviors will it reinforce—or erode?

- Are we designing for efficiency and belonging?

The Bottom Line

Culture isn't just built in town halls and values posters. It's lived in the daily friction (or flow) of how people work. Payroll, benefits, compliance, training, and development systems may seem like the "hard side," but they are the frontline of culture. Technology and process, when designed intentionally, can be the strongest allies of culture. When ignored, they can be culture's quietest enemies. The real opportunity lies in integrating the hard and soft sides of business, so they reinforce each other, creating a culture that is both high-performing and human-centered.

Culture is at once rational and emotional, measurable and intuitive, scientific and soulful. And that's exactly what makes it so powerful. Leaders who can embrace both sides are the ones who unlock cultures that not only drive business results but also create workplaces people are proud to call their own.

Reflection Questions:

1. Does your organization measure culture the same way it measures performance? Why or why not?
2. If you had to describe your culture in one word, would it be an emotion or a system? (And what does that tell you?)
3. Which side of culture feels stronger in your organization today — the science (systems, processes, metrics) or the soul (values, meaning, belonging)?

5

THE LEADERSHIP MANDATE

I'll never forget sitting in a boardroom with the leadership team of a company that had just gone through a painful restructuring. Morale was low, turnover was climbing, and employees were openly questioning whether the organization still lived its values.

The CEO began the meeting by saying something that stunned me:

"I know our strategy is strong, but if we can't get aligned as leaders, it won't matter. Our people won't follow us."

That moment was powerful because it was so rare. Most leaders I've worked with jump immediately to strategy, numbers, and market moves. Few pause long enough to recognize that strategy will never stand a chance without cultural alignment at the top.

And the CEO was right. Leadership alignment isn't a "soft" issue. It's the mandate.

Why Leadership Is the Culture

Employees don't experience culture as a mission statement on the wall. They experience it through leaders: in what they say, how they act, and where they focus their energy. A leader who praises results but ignores how they were achieved is telling everyone: "Outcomes matter more than values." A leader who avoids tough conversations signals that accountability is optional.

Gallup found that **70% of the variance in team engagement is attributable to the manager.** Culture, in other words, is not an idea. It's lived and felt through leadership behavior.

The Power of Alignment

One of the most revealing "culture tests" happens when the leadership team gathers. Do they show up aligned, reinforcing the same values and modeling consistent behaviors? Or do they operate as silos, each broadcasting their own version of "how we do things here"?

When leaders are fragmented, culture fractures. Employees receive competing signals, which leads to confusion, disengagement, and distrust. On the flip side, when leaders are aligned, culture becomes magnetic. Employees know what to expect, trust deepens, and the organization moves forward as one.

Harvard Business Review found that companies with aligned leadership teams are **1.9 times more likely to have above-average financial performance**. Alignment isn't cosmetic, it's foundational.

Patrick Lencioni, author of The Advantage, spoke of Leadership Team unification and its importance to organizational health and success. *"If an organization is led by a team that is not behaviorally unified, there is no chance that it will become healthy."*

The Cost of Misalignment

I once worked with a company where the CEO championed "innovation" as the organization's future. Yet other executives criticized employees for trying new things that didn't succeed. The result was predictable: innovation died before it even had a chance.

That disconnect wasn't just cultural, it was financial. Gallup estimates that disengaged employees cost U.S. companies **$450 to $550 billion annually** in lost productivity. Leadership misalignment is often the root cause.

The Leadership Mandate

So, what does this mandate require? It means leaders must:

- **Model** the culture every day in visible, tangible behaviors.

- **Align** with one another so employees see one consistent message.

- **Embed** culture into systems: hiring, recognition, promotions, performance reviews.

- **Communicate** the "why" of culture constantly, not just in town halls but in daily interactions.

- **Commit** to holding one another accountable when actions don't match values.

This isn't about charisma or perfection. It's about ownership. Leaders author culture — together.

Leadership Development is Flawed without Culture as its Guide

Companies spend billions on leadership development each year. Competency models, workshops, coaching, 360s, you name it. But too often, these investments don't move the needle.

I've been reflecting on this a lot lately. In past roles across different organizations, I've built Leadership Development programs grounded in competencies we identified as critical to each company's strategy.

We followed all the "right" steps:

- Used well-researched models and best practices
- Defined competencies in terms of clear, observable behaviors
- Involved executive leaders in gaining buy-in
- Launched with thoughtful, well-planned rollouts

And yet… the results often fell short.

Yes, some leaders completely engaged. They learned, grew, and took real ownership of their development, both personally and professionally. But those were individual successes, not systemic ones. While we saw growth in some leaders, we didn't see a unified elevation across the broader leadership team.

So, I began to ask: **What was missing?**
The answer: **CULTURE.**

Let's look at some common competencies:

- Strategic thinking
- Emotional intelligence
- Communication
- Decision-making

The problem is they're often too **generic**. They define what a good leader looks like in general, but not what *great leadership* looks like **here**, in **this organization**, with **these people**, driving **this strategy**.

Culture provides the WHY behind leadership behaviors. Here's the shift:

> Don't just teach *"decisiveness."*- Teach **why** quick decision-making is vital because your culture prizes agility and speed.

> Don't just teach *"collaboration."*- Teach **how** inclusive decision-making drives innovation in your values-driven, team-first culture.

Without that context, even great leaders may behave in ways that feel misaligned or confusing.

- **Audit your culture first:** Understand the real values and behaviors that guide how things get done.
- **Translate culture into competencies:** Define leadership behaviors that reflect and reinforce your unique culture.
- **Train with real context:** Use stories, situations, and case studies from your own organization, not theoretical scenarios.
- **Measure cultural alignment, not just skill building:** Evaluate whether leaders are building behaviors that support your actual way of working.

From HR Guardians to Leadership Architects

Too often, organizations hand culture to HR. When that happens, HR becomes a reactive "culture police," enforcing rules rather than enabling growth. HR's real role should be as a **strategic architect**, designing systems, building frameworks, and equipping leaders.

But the authors of culture? That's the leadership team. Every executive, every manager, and every team lead. When leaders step into this mandate, culture becomes a lived reality instead of a hollow aspiration.

Why This Matters More Than Ever

In today's hybrid, fast-changing workplace, culture is the anchor employees cling to. Deloitte reports that **94% of executives and 88% of employees believe a distinct workplace culture is critical to business success.**

So, the real question is no longer *"Does leadership own culture?"* The question is: *"How are leaders living that ownership today?"*

Culture doesn't live in slide decks or HR handbooks. It lives in the choices leaders make, the conversations they hold, and the courage they show.

When leaders embrace this mandate, not as a side project but as their most essential responsibility, culture transforms from a liability into a competitive advantage. And that's when strategy truly comes alive.

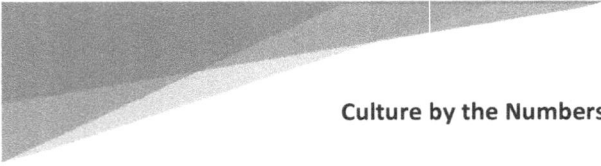

Culture by the Numbers

- **70%** of engagement variance is tied to managers (Gallup)

- **1.9x** better financial performance with aligned leadership (HBR)

- **$450–550B** lost each year to disengagement (Gallup)

- **94%** of leaders say culture drives success (Deloitte)

Reflection Questions:

1. If your employees were asked to describe your leadership team in one sentence, what would they say?
2. Do your leaders model a consistent message about culture, or are employees getting mixed signals?
3. Where are you, as a leader, unintentionally sending the wrong cultural signals? What would it look like to course-correct?

6
THE BLUEPRINT OF CULTURE

Several years ago, I worked with two companies in the same industry. On paper, they looked almost identical: similar size, similar customer base, similar strategy. One was growing rapidly, attracting top talent, and pulling ahead of competitors. The other was struggling with high turnover, flat growth, and declining engagement. Both had career frameworks, onboarding programs, and leadership training. Both invested heavily in engagement surveys. But only one treated culture as a system to be designed, built, and sustained. The other treated it as an afterthought.

That contrast is what set me on a mission. Over more than 25 years of driving organizational transformation, I kept asking the same question: why do well-intentioned initiatives (career frameworks, onboarding programs, leadership development) so often fail to deliver results? Gallup's State of the Global Workplace reports confirm what I was seeing: despite billions invested in engagement programs, global engagement has barely budged. Companies launch surveys, analyze data, and "hold managers accountable," yet fail to address the cultural foundations that shape how employees experience work every day.

The difference between struggling companies and thriving ones isn't strategy alone. It's intentionality. Too many HR leaders chase strategy, designing processes to support it. The most successful organizations do the opposite: they use culture to drive strategy. Research by Kotter and Heskett, along with decades of evidence from Denison Consulting, demonstrates that organizations with a clear purpose, aligned values, and disciplined cultural practices consistently outperform those that don't.

This is the foundation of the **Culture by Design Blueprint** ™. Like architecture, culture begins with a vision. That vision shapes the foundation, the framework, the systems, and the finishing details. The sequence matters: you can't put on a roof without first pouring a foundation. Skip steps, and the structure looks fine on the surface but can't support long-term growth. The same is true for building culture. There is a foundation followed by other commitments, processes, and systems to work in harmony.

This next section of the book lays out that blueprint. It organizes culture into three essential sets of elements:

- **Culture DNA**: the organization's core identity: its purpose, vision, and the values that guide progress.

- **Culture Commitments**: the mutual promises between the organization and its employees, including the behaviors that bring values to life.

- **Culture in Motion**: the rituals, processes, and feedback loops that embed culture into daily operations and ensure it evolves with the organization.

As Jim Collins reminds us, "good is the enemy of great." Too many organizations settle for good-enough culture, posters of values, annual surveys, or one-off programs, without building the discipline required for greatness. And as Patrick Lencioni has shown through his work on organizational health, the real competitive advantage comes from clarity, consistency, and courage.

The Culture by Design Blueprint gives leaders a way to bring that clarity and discipline to culture, transforming it from something abstract into the engine of strategy and the fuel for growth.

Below in Figure 1, you can see the simple template of the Culture by Design Blueprint ™. You can see the simple 9-box design. Each row represents a sequential element of culture: Culture DNA (top row), Culture Commitments (middle row), and Culture in Motion (bottom row). Across the foundation of the Blueprint is the Leadership Team as Role Models element which was discussed in the previous chapter and will be detailed again in the final section.

Culture™
by design

Culture DNA	Purpose: Why do we exist?	Vision: What future are we building toward?	Values: What do we believe will get us there? (top non-negotiable 3)
Culture Commitments	What do we promise to our people?	What do we expect from our people in return?	Behaviors: What do the Values look like in day-to-day activities?
Culture in Motion	Rituals: Weekly, Quarterly, Annual Focus on Values/Culture	Talent Management Processes:	Feedback and Evolution: How do we continuously listen and assess?
	Leadership Team as Role Models: Team of Leaders is united, collaborative and role models of culture.		

Figure 1: Culture by Design Blueprint

7
CULTURE DNA

The Foundation of Culture

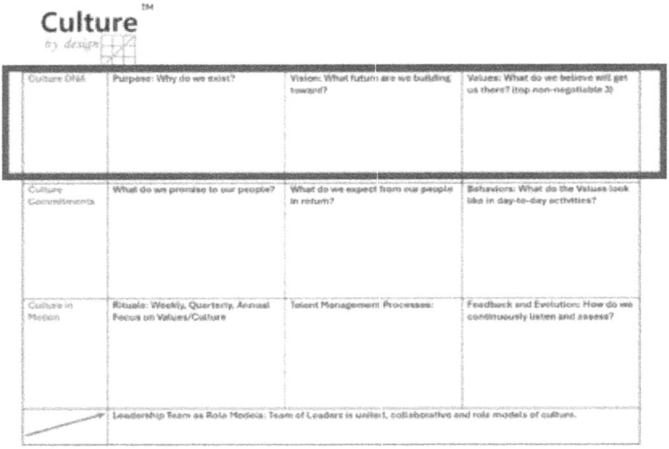

Culture™ by design

Culture DNA	Purpose: Why do we exist?	Vision: What future are we building toward?	Values: What do we believe will get us there? (top non-negotiable 3)
Culture Commitments	What do we promise to our people?	What do we expect from our people in return?	Behaviors: What do the Values look like in day-to-day activities?
Culture in Motion	Rituals: Weekly, Quarterly, Annual Focus on Values/Culture	Talent Management Processes:	Feedback and Evolution: How do we continuously listen and assess?
	Leadership Team as Role Models: Team of Leaders is united, collaborative and role models of culture.		

Every organization has a DNA, a set of defining elements that shape how people think, act, and decide. Just as biological DNA determines how living beings grow and function, cultural DNA determines how organizations evolve. It encodes identity, direction, and values. Whether leaders acknowledge it or not, every company has culture DNA. The question is: is it designed with intention, or is it left to chance?

Gallup's research makes this clear: employees who feel connected to their company's purpose are four times more engaged. Yet Deloitte's Human Capital Trends survey found that fewer than 50% of employees believe their organization's purpose actually guides decision-making. That gap between what's written on the wall and what's lived in the hall is often where culture falters.

The Culture by Design Blueprint begins with clarifying and codifying culture DNA. Without it, everything else, commitments, rituals, systems, rests on shaky ground.

Culture DNA consists of three core components:

- Purpose: Why do we exist?

- Vision: Where are we going?

- Values: What do we believe will get us there?

Purpose: The "Why" That Inspires

Simon Sinek popularized the phrase Start with Why, but the idea is timeless. Purpose answers the existential question: why does this organization exist beyond making money? Companies with a clear and compelling purpose don't just attract customers; they attract people who want to be part of something bigger than themselves.

Take Patagonia. Its purpose, we're in business to save our home planet, doesn't just live on a website—it drives decisions, from supply chain choices to employee activism. Contrast that with organizations where purpose is written by a marketing team, tucked into a brochure, and forgotten. One fuels loyalty and action, the other fuels cynicism.

For leaders, purpose is not about clever wording. It's about clarity and conviction. If leaders can't explain why the company exists in a sentence, employees will fill in the blank themselves, often with "to make money for shareholders."

Deepening Your Culture DNA with Purpose

Purpose promises meaning at a collective level, but does every person in the organization *see* how their daily work connects to that purpose? It's one thing to hang a mission on the wall; it's another for each employee to feel, in their role, that their work matters. Research shows that this sense of meaning has real impact. According to BetterUp Labs, employees who consider their work "very meaningful" contribute an extra **hour per week**, take **two fewer sick days per year**, and drive **$5,437 more in value per**

worker annually. Remarkably, according to SHRM, they're **69% less likely to resign** in the next six months and stay an average of **7.4 months longer** than employees who feel their work lacks meaning.

For today's workforce, particularly younger professionals, purpose isn't optional. A 2025 survey by Deloitte found that **89% of Gen Z** and **92% of millennials** say a sense of purpose is critical to their job satisfaction and well-being.

In other words: purpose only matters when each team member sees how their daily contributions connect to a larger, shared cause. As Culture Architects, our job is to close that gap, making purpose tangible in every role, reinforcing it in every conversation, and celebrating its impact daily.

Reflection questions for leaders:

- Why does our organization exist beyond profit?

- What problem in the world would not be solved if we ceased to exist?

- Does our purpose inspire employees and customers—or could it belong to any company?

- Can every employee on your team clearly explain how their work connects to the company's purpose?

Vision: The Destination That Guides

If purpose is the "why," vision is the "where." It paints a picture of the future state: what the organization is building toward. Vision brings focus. It acts like the North Star, helping employees align daily actions to long-term outcomes.

Collins and Porras, in Built to Last, call this a "Big Hairy Audacious Goal" (BHAG), a clear and compelling destination that challenges and unites. Think of SpaceX: to make humanity multiplanetary. Whether you agree with it or not, the clarity of vision focuses innovation, risk-taking, and resilience.

But clarity is not enough. Employees will only commit to a vision if they believe their leaders genuinely believe it themselves. Leaders must communicate vision with authenticity and conviction, showing not only that the destination is possible but also that they are personally invested in getting there. Inspiration comes not from perfectly polished words, but from leaders who visibly connect the vision to their own values and actions.

When a leader speaks about vision with energy and belief, it becomes contagious. When they speak about it as a corporate formality, it falls flat. Vision dies not because people disagree with it, but because they can't see their leaders bringing it to life.

Organizations without vision drift. Their strategies change with leadership turnover. Employees struggle to connect today's work with tomorrow's future. Without vision, even high engagement can become wasted energy, lots of motion, little progress.

When Vision and Culture Align

When vision and culture are in sync, the results are powerful:

- **Clarity of direction**: People understand not just *what* the company is trying to achieve, but *how* to contribute in meaningful ways.
- **Consistency in behavior**: Leaders and employees alike act in ways that reinforce shared goals and values.
- **Stronger engagement**: People feel connected to a larger purpose and to each other.
- **Faster, better decisions**: Teams are empowered to act because they understand the cultural guardrails and strategic priorities.

It's no coincidence that the most admired companies in the world, those known for both performance and employee loyalty, have a strong alignment between vision and culture.

Where It Breaks Down

Problems arise when vision and culture drift apart. Here are a few common disconnects:

- A beautifully crafted vision statement that doesn't influence real decisions or behaviors
- Legacy cultures that no longer serve the future the company is trying to build
- Leaders who unintentionally model behaviors that contradict the stated vision
- Systems (like hiring, recognition, or performance reviews) that reinforce old norms

In these cases, culture becomes a barrier, not a bridge, to growth.

Reflection questions for leaders:

- Where are we going in the next 5–10 years?

- What does success look like when we get there?

- Is our vision bold enough to inspire, yet clear enough to guide decisions?

- Am I modeling passion and commitment to this vision in my own actions?

A great vision is essential. But it's your culture, the collective behavior of your people, that will determine whether that vision comes to life.

When the two are aligned, you create not only a clear path forward but also an environment where people want to walk that path with you. That's how companies build legacies. That's how they grow sustainably, intentionally, and together.

Values: The Beliefs That Shape Behavior

So, let's shift to the third piece of your Culture's DNA – Values. Values are the "how." They describe the principles and standards that guide daily choices and interactions. Done right, values are the behavioral compass of an organization. Done poorly, they are platitudes, generic words like "integrity" or "teamwork" that could hang in any lobby.

When you visit a doctor, one of the first things they do is check your heart. A stethoscope to the chest, a hand on the pulse the heartbeat tells a story. Its rhythm reveals health, stress, resilience, and sometimes early warning signs that something deeper needs attention.

The same is true for organizations. If you want to know the true health of a business, you don't start with the balance sheet or the strategy deck, you start with its culture. And at the heart of culture are its **values**.

Just as the heartbeat keeps the human body aligned, flowing, and alive, values keep a business moving with clarity and purpose. They are the rhythm that guides how people behave, decide, and interact when no one is watching.

Unfortunately, too many companies treat values like decorations printed on posters, added to the website, or mentioned at town halls but rarely lived. That's like checking someone's heartbeat once a year and ignoring the signs in between. A true health check requires more.

Patrick Lencioni puts it bluntly: "If you're not willing to be punished for living a value, it's not really a value, it's an aspiration." In other words, values matter only when they shape real trade-offs. Netflix, for instance, is unapologetic about its value of "Performance." They use it to guide hiring, firing, and promotion, even when it means letting go of employees who are competent but not high-performing. That's not just a slogan; it's a cultural standard.

Values without behaviors are too vague to be actionable. Leaders must translate each value into observable, teachable, and measurable behaviors. For example, a company that values "Collaboration" might define it as:

- We proactively share information rather than hoarding it.

- We invite diverse perspectives before making major decisions.

- We celebrate team wins before individual ones.

When values are this concrete, they stop being posters and start being practiced.

Reflection questions for leaders:

- Which values are truly non-negotiable for us?

- Can we describe what each value looks like in behavior?

- Are we willing to hire, reward, and fire based on these values?

Bringing Culture DNA to Life

Purpose, vision, and values form the DNA of culture. But like real DNA, they don't function in isolation. They express themselves only when activated. This means leaders must embed them everywhere: strategy documents, hiring practices, performance systems, recognition programs, and daily rituals.

The key test of culture DNA is simple:

- Ask ten employees why the organization exists, where it's headed, and what it values.

- If you get ten different answers, your DNA isn't clear enough.

- If you get ten aligned answers that echo leadership's intent, you've built a strong foundation.

Closing Thought

As Jim Collins reminds us, "You can't predict the future, but you can create it." And Patrick Lencioni warns, "Culture eats strategy for breakfast only when it's left undefined." Purpose, vision, and values, the Culture DNA, give leaders the clarity to create a future worth building.

But clarity alone is not enough. For culture DNA to take root, leaders must believe it themselves and communicate it in ways that inspire others to believe too. Employees don't just need to understand the purpose, vision, and values, they need to feel that their leaders are convinced, committed, and passionate about them.

When leaders speak with conviction and act with consistency, the DNA becomes more than words on paper; it becomes a living force in the organization. That belief, communicated with authenticity and inspiration, is what transforms culture from abstract ideas into the foundation of strategy and the fuel for growth.

8

CULTURE COMMITMENTS

Turning DNA Into Promises

Culture™

If Culture DNA defines who we are, our purpose, vision, and values, then Culture Commitments define what we promise. They are the lived agreements between the organization and its people, the explicit give-and-take that turns identity into daily reality.

Commitments are more than employee handbooks or corporate slogans. They represent the mutual expectations that bind leaders and employees together: what the company offers its people, what it expects in return, and the behaviors everyone must live by to bring values to life.

When these commitments are clear, employees know where they stand and what matters most. When they are absent, or worse, when they are inconsistent, employees fill the void with assumptions, mistrust, or disengagement.

Why Commitments Matter

Research consistently shows that clarity of expectations is one of the strongest drivers of engagement. Gallup's State of the American Workplace study found that only about half of employees strongly agree they know what is expected of them at work. Those who do are 2.5 times more likely to be engaged. The takeaway is simple: ambiguity kills commitment.

Patrick Lencioni often says that organizational health is about creating clarity and overcommunicating it. Culture Commitments are exactly that: the clarity of what we promise, expect, and require. Without them, even the best purpose and vision risk collapsing under the weight of confusion and inconsistency.

Three Dimensions of Commitments

Culture Commitments can be organized into three dimensions:

1. **What We Promise Our People**

    This includes the tangible and intangible commitments an organization makes to employees: how they will be treated, supported, and developed. Promises might include providing meaningful work, opportunities for growth, a safe and inclusive environment, or recognition of contributions.

    o   Example: Southwest Airlines promises employees stability, appreciation, and a fun, people-first culture. That commitment underpins their legendary customer service.

2. **What We Expect in Return**

    Commitments are mutual. Organizations must be explicit about what they require from employees in exchange: accountability, performance, living the values, and contributing to the mission.

    o   Example: Netflix famously tells employees, "We're a team, not a family." The expectation is clear: bring your best performance, or you may not stay on the team. It's not warm language, but it's honest and it drives alignment.

3. **The Behaviors That Bring Values to Life**

Values without behaviors are vague. Commitments must define what values look like in action. These behavioral commitments become the true cultural currency, shaping hiring, performance management, recognition, and leadership expectations.

- o Example: A company with "Innovation" as a value might commit to behaviors such as: "We experiment quickly, learn from failure, and share lessons openly."

The Danger of Implied Promises

One of the greatest risks in culture is the gap between stated commitments and implied commitments. Employees hear what leaders say, but they also infer commitments from what leaders reward, tolerate, or ignore. If a company says, "We value collaboration," but rewards individual achievement exclusively, the implied commitment is that collaboration doesn't really matter.

This is why alignment between words and actions is so critical. Research by the Edelman Trust Barometer shows that when employees perceive inconsistency between leadership's promises and behaviors, trust erodes rapidly, and trust, once broken, is hard to rebuild.

Bringing Commitments to Life

Culture Commitments only matter when they are visible and embedded. Leaders must:

- **Codify them**: Write them down clearly so there's no ambiguity.

- **Communicate them**: Overcommunicate through stories, examples, and repetition.

- **Model them**: Live them consistently as leaders—because employees notice what leaders do more than what they say.

- **Reinforce them**: Integrate commitments into hiring, performance reviews, recognition, and promotions.

As Collins reminds us, "People don't engage with what you hope for; they engage with what you commit to."

The Power of Commitments: Alignment and Self-Selection

Culture Commitments do more than clarify expectations, they act as a mirror for employees to see whether they fit within the organization. When commitments are clearly defined, employees can find alignment: they understand the behaviors, values, and performance standards expected, and can make conscious choices to engage, contribute, and thrive.

Equally important, commitments reveal misalignment. Not every talented employee is a cultural fit, and that's okay. When people see that their personal values or preferred ways of working conflict with the organization's commitments, they may self-select out. This is not a failure; it is a feature of intentional culture design. By surfacing alignment and misalignment early, commitments protect both the individual and the organization, preventing frustration, disengagement, and turnover later.

For example, Netflix's approach to high performance is famously transparent. Employees know that the company values accountability, candor, and exceptional contribution. Those who thrive under these expectations flourish; those who do not recognize the misalignment and often leave voluntarily. This creates a workforce that is not only capable but also culturally aligned, increasing cohesion, trust, and organizational energy.

Commitments are therefore a powerful tool for:

- Guiding alignment: helping employees understand how to succeed within the culture.

- Encouraging self-selection: enabling employees who do not fit to step away gracefully, preserving both individual and organizational well-being.

- Strengthening culture: ensuring that over time, the workforce is comprised of people who embody the organization's DNA, which amplifies engagement and performance.

When commitments are clear, employees don't have to guess if they "fit." They can make intentional decisions to stay, adapt, or move on, creating a healthier, more sustainable culture.

Reflection Questions for Leaders

- What promises are we making to employees, explicitly or implicitly?

- Are those promises realistic and sustainable?

- What do we expect from employees in return, and have we been clear about it?

- Have we defined values as specific, observable behaviors that anyone could recognize?

- Do our leaders model and reinforce these commitments daily?

Closing Thought

Culture Commitments are the bridge between an organization's DNA, its purpose, vision, and values, and the reality of daily work. They clarify what the organization promises, what it expects, and the behaviors that bring values to life.

But their true power lies in alignment. When commitments are clear and consistently modeled by leaders, employees can see where they fit and how to thrive. And just as importantly, commitments reveal misalignment, allowing individuals who do not share the organization's values or way of working to self-select out. This is not a failure, it is an intentional part of building a strong, cohesive culture.

As Lencioni shows, clarity and courage in leadership create organizational health. Culture Commitments give employees the clarity to align with the organization, or the insight to step away, ensuring that over time, the workforce is composed of people who truly belong. When this happens, culture becomes not just a statement of intent, but a living, self-reinforcing system that drives engagement, performance, and long-term success.

.

9
CULTURE IN MOTION

Making Culture Real

Culture™
by design

Culture DNA	Purpose: Why do we exist?	Vision: What future are we building toward?	Values: What do we believe will get us there? (top non-negotiable 3)
Culture Commitments	What do we promise to our people?	What do we expect from our people in return?	Behaviors: What do the Values look like in day-to-day activities?
Culture in Motion	Rituals: Weekly, Quarterly, Annual Focus on Values/Culture	Talent Management Processes:	Feedback and Evolution: How do we continuously listen and assess?

Leadership Team as Role Models: Team of Leaders is united, collaborative and role models of culture.

Purpose, vision, values, and commitments are essential, but they remain abstract unless they are embedded in day-to-day life. Culture in Motion is where strategy meets reality: the rituals, systems, and feedback mechanisms that make culture tangible, actionable, and sustainable.

Jim Collins famously observed that companies often fail not from bad strategy, but from poor execution. Patrick Lencioni reminds us that clarity is meaningless if it isn't reinforced consistently. Culture in Motion ensures that what's defined in DNA and Commitments is experienced by every employee, every day.

Without this step, culture risks becoming decorative: posters on walls, slogans in emails, or statements on a website. With it, culture becomes a living, breathing system that guides decisions, behaviors, and priorities.

The Three Pillars of Culture in Motion

1. **Rituals: Making Culture Visible**

   Rituals are repeated actions that signal what the organization values. They can be formal, like recognition ceremonies, town halls, or quarterly reviews, or informal, such as storytelling, shared celebrations, or rituals around onboarding.

   In the rush of business, we often focus on big things: strategies, structures, organizational charts. But culture lives in the small, repeated things: how meetings begin, how we recognize effort, how we mark transitions.

   These are rituals. And they're one of the most powerful, yet underutilized tools leaders have to turn company values into shared experience.

   Rituals do more than celebrate values. They reinforce them. For example, Zappos embeds "WOW" customer service into its culture through rituals like peer-to-peer recognition programs, culture committee events, and new-hire culture boot camps. Rituals are the social glue that make commitments lived experiences, not abstract ideals.

   Effective rituals are:

   - Repeatable
   - Emotionally resonant
   - Tied to a specific value
   - Created with employees, not for them
   - Easy to maintain (not another task to dread)

2. **Talent Management Processes: Embedding Culture in Systems**

   Recruitment, onboarding, performance management, promotions, and learning programs are levers for reinforcing culture. When aligned with Culture DNA and Commitments, these processes ensure that only people who fit and live the culture thrive, and that the culture evolves systematically.

For example:

- o Hiring: Interview questions and assessment criteria reflect both skills and alignment with values.

- o Performance management: Reviews measure not only outcomes but also behaviors that reflect commitments.

- o Learning & development: Programs reinforce desired capabilities and behaviors that bring culture to life.

Look a bit closer at **Onboarding** as an example:

Most organizations see onboarding as a checklist: forms to sign, systems to access, policies to review. But onboarding is more than orientation. Done well, it's the most powerful culture-shaping moment you have.

An intentional onboarding experience does more than explain "how things work." It immerses people into the why behind your organization, connecting them to your purpose, values, and vision.

When culture is woven into onboarding:

- Engagement soars: New hires understand how their work connects to the mission.
- Productivity ramps faster: They feel confident, connected, and equipped to contribute.
- Retention improves: People stay where they feel aligned, supported, and valued.

The biggest mistake organizations make is treating

onboarding as a one-time event, a single day or week that "checks the box." But culture, trust, and capability don't form in a single meeting or presentation.

When there's alignment in your Talent Management Processes it ensures culture isn't something employees passively adopt. It's embedded in the structure of work.

3. **Listening and Feedback: Keeping a Finger on the Pulse**

    Culture is dynamic. Regular feedback, surveys, focus groups, and one-on-one conversations allow leaders to understand how culture is experienced and where it may be drifting.

    But data alone isn't enough. Leaders must act on insights, communicate changes, and iterate. When employees see that feedback leads to visible action, trust grows, and culture strengthens. Conversely, ignoring feedback erodes credibility and engagement.

The Role of Leaders in Culture in Motion

Culture in Motion requires visible and consistent leadership. Leaders must:

- Model behaviors that reflect values and commitments.

- Celebrate examples of employees living the culture.

- Ensure that rituals and processes align with cultural intent.

- Respond to feedback and adapt when gaps are identified.

Collins and Lencioni agree leadership consistency is the most powerful driver of sustained culture. Employees watch what leaders do far more closely than what leaders say. Leaders' behaviors signal priorities, reinforce commitments, and keep the culture alive.

Reflection Questions for Leaders

- Which rituals consistently reinforce our Culture DNA and Commitments?

- Are our talent processes aligned with the behaviors and values we expect?

- How do we capture and act on feedback about culture experiences?

- Do our leaders visibly model and celebrate the culture daily?

Closing Thought

Culture in Motion transforms strategy into lived experience. It operationalizes the DNA and Commitments so that every employee sees, feels, and participates in the culture every day. It ensures alignment, provides feedback loops, and keeps the organization adaptive.

When culture is in motion, it becomes self-reinforcing. Employees understand not only what the organization expects but also how to act, where to focus energy, and how they fit, or don't fit, within the culture. This clarity accelerates engagement, drives performance, and strengthens the organization's ability to achieve its vision.

As Lencioni notes, clarity, consistency, and courage are the hallmarks of healthy organizations. Culture in Motion is how those qualities are brought to life. It is the operational heartbeat of the Culture by Design Blueprint, connecting DNA and Commitments to real-world outcomes, every day.

10
BECOMING A CULTURE ARCHITECT

Culture doesn't transform itself. It's shaped, deliberately or by default, through the mindsets and actions of leaders. Becoming a Culture Architect isn't just about building systems or designing processes. It starts with how you *think* about culture: the mindset you bring into the work.

Too often, leaders want to leap straight into solutions: a new engagement survey, a fresh set of values on the wall, a recognition program. But lasting culture change doesn't start with programs. It starts with courage, alignment, and intentional action.

The Three Mindsets of a Culture Architect

1. **Acknowledge**
   A true architect begins by looking at the foundation, not the paint on the walls. Becoming a culture architect requires the courage to accept the reality of your current state. Where are the cracks? Where are the disconnects between what your organization says it values are and what employees experience? Looking away only delays the inevitable. Acknowledging the truth, however uncomfortable, is the first act of leadership courage.

2. **Align**
   Culture cannot, and should not, be the sole responsibility of HR. To design culture with intention, you must align with your executive team. This means co-creating the blueprint: sharing authorship, commitments, and ownership. Alignment is not about unanimous agreement on every detail; it's about unified clarity on the vision and consistency in how you show up.

3. **Act**
   A plan without action is just a wish. The final mindset shift is about deliberate, intentional action and, at times, personal behavior change. Culture-driving actions must be placed at the same level (and sometimes a higher level) of priority as business-driving

actions. Strategy may set the destination, but it's your daily behaviors, decisions, and rituals that pave the road to get there.

When leaders embrace these three mindsets, **acknowledge, align, act**, they move from being managers of culture to true architects of it. Only then can the blueprints you design turn into a living, breathing culture that shapes performance, engagement, and impact.

The Blueprint Process

Mindsets set the stage but process builds the structure. Just as an architect moves from vision to design to execution, so too must leaders who want to intentionally shape culture. The blueprint process includes five steps:

1. **Assessing the Current State**
   Surveys, interviews, and focus groups help you understand what's strong, what's weak, and where disconnects exist.

2. **Strategizing/Deeper Dive**
   Explore microcultures, identify friction points, and uncover the "why" of culture. What business outcomes will be strengthened if culture shifts? Where will alignment pay off most?

3. **Designing**
   Use the blueprint as a guide to sketch the ideal state. This begins with defining your **Culture DNA** (the core identity), then creating **Culture Commitments** (the shared promises and behaviors), and finally mapping **Culture in Motion** (implementation plans that turn commitments into action).

4. **Implementing**
   Translate design into practice by modeling, embedding, and reinforcing culture in every system, process, and behavior.

5. **Sustaining**
   Culture is never "finished." The final step is about continuous reinforcement, accountability, and renewal so that culture evolves alongside your business.

This combination of **mindset and method** is what allows leaders to move from aspiration to action, from culture by chance to culture by design.

Reflection Questions

- **Acknowledge:** Where are the cracks in your culture today that you may be hesitant to name out loud? What's one uncomfortable truth you need to face?

- **Align:** How aligned is your executive team on culture? Where do you see mixed messages or competing priorities?

- **Act:** What's one behavior you personally need to change if you want to model the culture you want to see in others?

11
STEP ONE: ASSESSING THE CURRENT STATE

Every cultural journey begins with a mirror. Before leaders can design the future, they must first face the reality of today. That's what assessment is all about: holding up a clear, honest reflection of your organization's culture as it actually exists, not as you hope it exists, or as it appears in a strategy deck.

Too often, companies skip this step. They leap straight into defining values, creating slogans, or launching recognition programs, all without pausing to ask: *What's really going on here?* The result is a disconnect between the aspirational culture leaders want to see and the lived experience employees actually feel.

Why Assessment Matters

Research underscores this need for clarity. According to Gallup, only **27% of employees strongly believe in their company's values** and even fewer say they see those values consistently lived out. Deloitte has found that organizations with intentionally measured and aligned cultures are **three times more likely to achieve high performance.** Assessment isn't a "nice-to-have"; it's the foundation for everything that follows.

Think of it this way: if you were renovating a home, you wouldn't start by picking paint colors. You'd bring in an inspector to check the foundation, wiring, and plumbing. Culture works the same way. Without an honest inspection, you risk building on cracks you can't see.

Three Dimensions of Cultural Assessment

A robust cultural assessment explores three layers:

1. **Perceptions (What people feel and say).**
    Surveys, pulse checks, and employee engagement scores help capture broad sentiment. Questions might ask: "Do you believe

leadership lives the company values?" or "Do you feel proud to work here?" While numbers give you trends, open-ended survey questions often reveal the stories behind the data.

2. **Experiences (What people actually encounter).**
Interviews and focus groups uncover the lived experience: how decisions are made, how conflict is handled, whether promotions feel fair, and how leaders show up day-to-day. This qualitative insight provides the richness that surveys alone cannot capture.

3. **Behaviors and Systems (What the organization rewards and reinforces).**
Look at performance reviews, recognition programs, promotions, and policies. Do they reward collaboration or competition? Risk-taking or risk avoidance? The systems and structures in place often reveal more about the *real* culture than the words on a wall.

Looking for Cracks and Strengths

When assessing culture, you're searching for two things:

- **Cracks:** points of friction, misalignment, or hypocrisy. For example, a company that champions "innovation" but punishes failure will reveal a cultural crack.
- **Strengths:** existing cultural elements worth preserving or amplifying. Perhaps your teams already collaborate brilliantly across departments, or your frontline employees consistently go above and beyond for customers.

Assessment is not just about finding problems; it's about identifying the raw material you want to keep and build upon.

A Story from the Field

I once worked with a growing tech firm whose leaders believed their culture was "collaborative, innovative, and fun." But when we conducted interviews and surveys, employees painted a very different picture. Collaboration was inconsistent: some teams thrived, while others operated in silos. Innovation was discussed at all-hands meetings but rarely rewarded in performance reviews. And "fun" meant different things depending on whether you worked in headquarters or a remote office.

The takeaway? There wasn't one culture, there were many microcultures. Leaders hadn't faced this reality until the assessment made it visible. Once they acknowledged the disconnects, they could begin aligning on what truly mattered across the company.

Another Story from the Field

At one technical company, "Exceptional Service" was declared a core value. Yet in practice, Sales and Installation were anything but aligned. Sales, driven by commissions, closed deals that weren't technically feasible, leaving installers to face frustrated customers and failed promises. The rift between the two teams grew, and collaboration broke down.

What leadership eventually realized was that this wasn't just a process issue, it was a cultural crack showing itself. Disruptions between teams are often informal assessments of culture. When people clash, when frustration bubbles up, it's usually a sign that the stated values and the lived behaviors don't match.

By bringing Sales, Installation, and Compensation leaders together, the company was able to address both the process and the cultural disconnect. Sales had to confirm technical feasibility before closing deals, and commissions were tied to successful installations. With those shifts, trust was rebuilt, the value of "Exceptional Service" became real, and culture was strengthened through aligned behaviors.

Lesson learned: Cultural cracks don't always show up in surveys. They often appear in the daily friction between teams. Paying attention to those moments can reveal where your culture needs repair.

How to Approach Assessment with Courage

Assessing culture takes courage, because it will surface truths leaders may not want to hear. Some employees may express cynicism. Others may reveal ways in which leadership unintentionally undermines the very values it promotes. But this discomfort is where transformation begins.

The role of the culture architect is not to spin the data into a "rosy picture," but to help the organization tell the truth about itself, so it can grow into something stronger.

Reflection Questions

- What tools are we currently using (surveys, interviews, focus groups) to assess our culture? Where are the gaps?
- When was the last time we asked employees about their lived experiences, not just their engagement levels?
- What cracks in our culture do we already suspect exist — and do we have the courage to name them openly?
- What cultural strengths do we most want to preserve and amplify?

12
STEP TWO: STRATEGIZE/TAKING A DEEPER DIVE

If Step One is about holding up the mirror, Step Two is about leaning in closer. A surface-level cultural snapshot will show you trends, but it rarely captures the nuances that actually make or break an organization's cultural health. This is where the deeper dive comes in.

At this stage, you move beyond broad sentiment to explore the subtleties: the microcultures, the unspoken "rules," and the friction points that quietly drain energy or block progress. Just as a doctor doesn't stop at a stethoscope reading but runs deeper tests to understand the whole patient, leaders must probe deeper to understand the full story of their culture.

Discovering Microcultures

Every organization has microcultures, the unique "mini-cultures" that form within teams, departments, or geographies. Some are powerful strategy accelerators, while others pull in the opposite direction.

A Deloitte study found that nearly **70% of employees say their team culture is more important to them than their overall organizational culture.** This means leaders can't assume a single "culture" exists; they need to map the variations across the enterprise.

For example, in a financial services firm I supported, the sales division operated in a highly competitive, individualistic culture, while the operations team prized stability and collaboration. Neither was "wrong," but the friction between the two created constant tension in service delivery. Acknowledging those differences was the first step to finding a shared cultural language.

Microcultures don't just live in frontline teams or specific departments, they can form even at the executive level. In fact, one of the most dangerous fractures in culture can occur when the senior leadership team itself operates as multiple "mini cultures." For example, the CFO may prioritize financial discipline above all else, while the Chief Revenue Officer pushes for aggressive growth, and the CHRO champions people-first practices. Each leader may be consistent within their own silo, but together they fail to model one unified culture.

Patrick Lencioni describes this challenge in his concept of *Team One*. His point is clear: the most important team for any executive is not the team they directly lead, but the executive team they sit on. When executives put loyalty to their own functions above loyalty to the collective leadership group, they unintentionally signal to the rest of the organization that alignment is optional. That fractures culture from the very top.

The truth is, microcultures at the executive level ripple outward with greater force than those in any other part of the organization. If the senior team models cohesion, commitment, and clarity, those behaviors cascade. If they model division and competition, that cascades too. Leaders must therefore recognize that cultural alignment starts with them, living as *Team One* first, so that the entire organization can follow.

Surfacing Points of Friction

The deeper dive also means identifying **where culture creates drag.**

- Are there bottlenecks in decision-making?

- Do employees feel excluded from opportunities or conversations?

- Are espoused values contradicted by everyday practices?

Harvard Business Review research shows that when employees perceive cultural hypocrisy, leaders say one thing but reward another, trust drops by more than **50%.** This erosion of trust quickly undermines engagement and performance.

Connecting Culture to the "Why"

The other critical layer of Step Two is meaning. It's not enough to say, "Our culture is broken" or "We want a better culture." Leaders must connect culture to **business outcomes and strategic priorities.**

Ask:

- How will aligning culture improve customer experience?

- How will it accelerate innovation or speed to market?

- How will it reduce turnover or increase engagement?

When leaders articulate the "why," culture work stops feeling like a soft initiative and starts becoming a business imperative. As one CEO I worked with put it: *"We don't work on culture for culture's sake. We work on it because it fuels growth, resilience, and trust."*

The Courage to Look Deeper

Taking this deeper dive isn't always comfortable. Microcultures can reveal inequities or silos leaders didn't realize existed. Friction points may point directly back to executive behavior. And the "why" may challenge leaders to admit they've prioritized short-term wins over long-term health.

But this is the essence of the culture architect's role: to help leaders see clearly, align on meaning, and build the courage to move forward together.

Applying Assessment to the Culture by Design Blueprint

When you apply the Culture by Design Blueprint, the first thing you do is map the results of your assessments, both the formal surveys and the informal pulse checks, onto each Culture Element. This creates a snapshot of the culture as it really is: where it's strong, where it's fragile, and how the different elements connect.

Case Example:

I remember working with one company that was especially proud
of its talent management processes. In our very first meeting, the
CHRO leaned across the table and said confidently, "If there's one
thing we do well, it's talent. We've got solid performance reviews,
promotion criteria, and a development program that people line up
for."

On the surface, they weren't wrong. The systems were all there,
polished and well-documented. But when we ran their culture
assessments through the blueprint, an uncomfortable truth came
into focus. Their values, the foundation of the culture, were vague.
When I asked employees to describe them, most hesitated. Some
recited words from a poster on the wall. A few admitted quietly,
"I'm not really sure what they mean for me day to day."

So, in the next leadership session, I put the blueprint up on the
screen and said, "Here's the issue: you believe your strength is
talent management. But values come first in the blueprint. They are
what inform the behaviors you hire for, develop, and reward. If
your values aren't clear or lived, how can they possibly be infused
into your processes?"

The room went quiet. One executive finally broke the silence: "So
you're saying we've been building on sand?"

"Exactly," I replied. "Your processes look strong, but without a
clear foundation of values, they don't hold. That's why employees
experience inconsistency. What you think is a strength is really a
crack, and the blueprint has just revealed it."

It was a sobering moment, but also a powerful one. The leadership
team realized they had to go back and do the hard work of
clarifying and embedding their values before their talent systems
could truly deliver. And once they did, everything began to align:
their processes became more than systems; they became
expressions of who they were as a company.

That's the power of mapping your culture with the blueprint: it doesn't just show you where you are; it reveals the hidden truths about why things do, or don't, work the way you think they do.

Reflection Questions

- What microcultures exist within our organization, and how do they align — or conflict — with our enterprise culture?

- Where are the biggest points of cultural friction, and how do they affect performance or employee experience?

- Have we clearly articulated *why* culture matters to our business success right now?

- Are we prepared to have uncomfortable conversations about the deeper truths our culture assessment reveals?

- As an executive, do you see your primary team as your functional area (Finance, HR, Sales, etc.) or as the collective leadership team?

- Where might our executive team unintentionally be sending mixed cultural messages to the organization?

- What would it look like if we truly operated as a Unified Leadership Team? What behaviors would need to change?

- How are we holding ourselves accountable to shared commitments — not just individual or departmental goals?

- If someone outside the executive team were observing our interactions, what culture would they see us modeling?

13
STEP THREE: DESIGNING WITH EXECUTIVE AUTHORSHIP

Culture cannot be delegated. It is written, spoken, and lived by leaders, or it doesn't exist at all. While HR leaders, consultants, and culture champions can facilitate the work, the actual authorship belongs to the executive team. Without their voice and conviction, culture becomes just another program, doomed to fade when the next priority emerges.

When executives step into authorship, they don't just approve language drafted by someone else. They write it, own it, and carry it. They become the storytellers and the standard-bearers, modeling the choices, trade-offs, and commitments that bring culture to life.

Patrick Lencioni describes this as leaders being "the chief reminding officers." But even more than reminding, executives must be authors, the ones who decide what story is being told, and what future is being written.

It's essential to bring the executive leadership team together at this stage. If you've already completed Steps 1 and 2—assessing your current culture and taking a deeper look at potential cracks—the next move is to share your insights with the entire executive team. Use the Blueprint as a guide to highlight both strengths and opportunities. Then, create space for the team to reflect and discuss the current state. Keep in mind: acknowledging reality is the foundation for any meaningful progress.

Authorship Begins with the DNA

The Culture by Design Blueprint starts with Culture DNA: purpose, vision, and values. These elements form the foundation of everything else.

- Purpose answers why we exist.
- Vision answers where we are going and what's possible.
- Values answer who we are and how we behave along the way.

When executives write these themselves, arguing over words, testing ideas against reality, and declaring what matters, they move beyond slogans.

They produce DNA that is authentic and durable.

Jim Collins' research reinforces this: enduring companies are anchored by clear core values and a sense of purpose that remain constant even as strategies and practices evolve. Without executives owning this foundation, culture is left unstable.

It's worth emphasizing that most companies already have mission, vision, and values statements in place. What matters now is for the executive leadership team to revisit these and align—reflecting the second mindset of a Culture Architect—on a shared understanding of these core DNA elements. If alignment is missing, the DNA must be refined or even redefined.

The Bridge: Culture Commitments

Once the DNA is defined, the next step is translating it into Culture Commitments, the bridge between belief and behavior.

Culture Commitments answer two critical questions:

1. What do leaders promise employees?

2. What do leaders expect in return?

But commitments go beyond promises. They also serve as the translation mechanism between values and behaviors. If values are the principles we claim to believe in, commitments define how those principles must show up in action, not as suggestions, but as non-negotiable standards for how people work together.

For example:

- If the value is Integrity, the commitment might be: *"We will tell the truth, even when it costs us. In return, we expect you to speak up when you see something wrong."*

- If the value is Collaboration, the commitment could be: *"We will reward team success over individual heroics. In return, we expect you to share credit and information openly."*

- If the value is Excellence, the commitment might be: *"We will provide the resources for you to do great work. In return, we expect you to own the quality of what you deliver."*

These statements are powerful because they transform values from abstract ideals into collective, behavioral commitments, clear expectations of "this is how we do things here."

Commitments as Collective, Non-Negotiable Behaviors

When executives write commitments, they are not just drafting lofty words. They are defining the non-negotiables, the minimum shared standards that everyone in the organization, from the C-suite to the front line, must live by.

These are not optional or personality-based preferences; they are the behaviors required to belong to the culture. For instance:

- "We return calls to customers within 24 hours."

- "We don't gossip; we address conflict directly."

- "We challenge ideas, not people."

- "We start meetings on time."

These may seem simple, but they are the daily actions that prove whether a culture's DNA is alive or not.

The power of commitments lies in their clarity. They allow employees to quickly understand what is celebrated, what is tolerated, and what is unacceptable. They also create fairness, everyone is held to the same bar, regardless of role or tenure.

The Courage of Authorship

For executives, this stage is often the most uncomfortable. Writing commitments forces them to confront whether they themselves live the values. A leader who values autonomy may resist a collaboration commitment. Another who thrives on recognition may hesitate to reward team outcomes over individual ones.

That tension is not a problem, it is the work. As commitments are clarified, alignment (or lack thereof) is revealed. Leaders must decide: are they truly willing to model these non-negotiables, or are they unwilling to author a culture they cannot embody?

Sometimes this process even leads to self-selection out. An executive may step aside, recognizing that the culture being authored is not one they can authentically champion. As hard as that feels, it is a win for the organization because a culture with misaligned authors is one destined to fracture.

Commitments as a Contract

When completed, Culture Commitments become a kind of social contract, a two-way agreement between leaders and employees that holds weight across the entire organization. Unlike posters or slogans, commitments are lived daily and reinforced collectively.

- Leaders are accountable for keeping their promises.

- Employees are accountable for living the behaviors.

- Both sides know the commitments are not aspirational, they are required.

This is why commitments are so critical: they ensure values don't stay trapped in the abstract but are translated into clear, collective, non-negotiable behaviors that shape the real employee experience.

Case Story: Commitments That Exposed the Gap

I once worked with a company that proudly declared collaboration as one of its core values. On paper, it looked inspiring. Posters in the hallways carried the word. Employees wore lanyards with the value printed on them.

But when I pressed the executive team to define the commitments behind it, the silence was deafening.

Would they promise employees that decisions would always be transparent? Would they commit to rewarding team success over individual heroics? Would they expect employees to share credit, not hoard it?

The room grew tense. A few executives admitted quietly that they weren't sure they could live those commitments, they preferred autonomy and individual recognition. At that moment, the gap was exposed: the value they claimed was not the value they were willing to author.

Rather than gloss over the tension, we held it. After several uncomfortable conversations, the team came to a decision: "If we can't make this commitment, then collaboration isn't truly one of our values."

That moment of honesty changed everything. They redefined their DNA, clarified their commitments, and employees immediately felt the shift. For the first time, the organization's values and behaviors aligned.

This is the power of executive authorship: it reveals whether leaders are willing to back their words with promises and behaviors, or whether they are content to let culture stay shallow.

Culture in Motion

Once DNA and commitments are in place, executives must ensure culture moves beyond words, into action. This is where Culture in Motion comes in: the rituals, processes, and feedback loops that embed culture into daily life.

1. Rituals

- A tech company opens every weekly meeting with a "customer win" story, reinforcing its value of customer focus.

- A consulting firm has a tradition of senior leaders writing handwritten notes of appreciation for employees who modeled values that week.

- A healthcare organization pauses at the start of every shift to ask, "How will we demonstrate care today?"

Rituals make culture visible.

2. Talent Processes

- Recruitment and promotion criteria are tied explicitly to values. Candidates are asked not only about skills, but about how they have lived behaviors tied to commitments.

- Performance reviews include a "how" dimension, evaluating whether results were achieved in alignment with cultural expectations.

- Recognition programs reward values-driven behavior, not just outcomes.

Processes make culture systematic.

3. Ongoing Feedback

- Pulse surveys track whether employees feel commitments are real.

- Listening sessions give employees space to share whether rituals and processes align with stated values.

- Leaders share back what they heard—and what will change as a result.

Feedback keeps culture honest.

When executives visibly own these practices, culture shifts from a static declaration to a living system.

The Executive Litmus Test

To know whether executives are truly acting as authors, ask:

- Can they explain purpose, vision, and values in their own words without a script?

- Do employees hear commitments modeled in executive decisions, not just in HR policies?

- Are rituals and processes visibly shaped by leaders, not delegated away?

- Do employees see leaders as both believers in the vision and enforcers of the commitments?

If the answers are "yes," then culture has been authored. If not, executives are still only editing someone else's draft.

The Payoff of Authorship

When executives co-author culture DNA, commitments, and culture in motion, the payoff is unmistakable:

- Trust—employees believe leaders mean what they say.

- Clarity—values and commitments guide real choices.

- Consistency—rituals and processes reinforce, rather than contradict, the culture.

- Engagement—employees feel connected because they know what to expect and what is expected of them.

- Resilience—culture becomes a stabilizing force when strategies shift or external pressures rise.

In the end, designing with executive authorship transforms culture from a set of words into a living, breathing system, anchored by DNA, upheld by commitments, and kept in motion through everyday practices.

Reflection & Practice: Becoming Culture Authors

This chapter has shown why executives must become authors of culture—owning the DNA, defining commitments, and putting culture in motion. The following prompts and exercises are designed for executive teams to use together. They help surface alignment, expose gaps, and create the courage to commit.

1. Reflect on Authorship

- Can you personally state your organization's purpose, vision, and values without looking at a document?

- When employees think of your culture, do they hear your voice, or HR's voice?

- Have you ever made a decision that contradicted the stated values? How did you handle it?

Exercise: In pairs, take five minutes each to articulate your organization's purpose, vision, and values in your own words. Compare notes. Where do you align? Where do your words differ? What does that difference reveal?

---

2. Translate Values into Commitments

- Choose one of your values. Ask: "What do we promise employees around this value?"

- Then ask: "What do we expect in return?"

- Finally, ask: "What behaviors must be non-negotiable if this value is real here?"

Exercise: As a team, create a chart with three columns:

1. Value

2. Our Promise to Employees

3. Our Expectation in Return

4. Non-Negotiable Behaviors

Fill it out for each value. Then ask yourselves: Are we willing to live this, even when it costs us?

---

3. Spot the Cracks

- Where do your current processes or rituals look "strong on paper" but crack under the weight of unclear values or weak commitments?

- Which commitments feel authentic and doable, and which feel hollow or aspirational?

Exercise: Review one current talent process (e.g., performance reviews, promotions, recognition). Identify:

- How is it aligned with values and commitments?

- Where does it contradict or ignore them?

- What one change would make it reinforce your authored culture?

4. Culture in Motion Audit

- What are your existing rituals (big or small)? Do they reinforce or dilute your culture?

- Which talent processes currently reward or punish alignment with values?

- Where do you invite ongoing feedback about culture, and how often do employees see you act on it?

Exercise: With your team, create a list of three rituals, three processes, and three feedback loops in your company. For each, rate them on a scale of 1–5:

- 1 = undermines our culture

- 3 = neutral, no real impact

- 5 = reinforces our culture powerfully

Commit to redesigning at least one "1" into a "5."

5. The Courage Check

- Which commitment is hardest for you, personally, to live consistently?

- If the culture you are authoring demands it, are you willing to change—or would you rather step aside?

Exercise: Silent reflection: write down one behavior you know you must model better for your commitments to be real. Then share it with the team. Invite the team to hold you accountable.

Closing Thought

Culture authorship is not about perfect words—it is about lived conviction. Executives who write their culture together define their non-negotiable commitments and embed them into motion create a culture that employees can believe in, trust, and live every day.

14
STEP FOUR: IMPLEMENTING CULTURE BY DESIGN

Designing culture on paper is important, but it's not the finish line, it's the starting line. Many organizations make the mistake of believing a vision statement, values refresh or set of culture commitments will somehow "take hold" on their own. But culture doesn't live in posters on the wall or words on a website. It lives in action. Implementation is where culture comes to life, or dies quietly from neglect.

The Power of Intentional Implementation

Implementation requires leaders to model, reinforce, and embed cultural commitments into everyday operations. Gallup research has found that only **27% of employees strongly believe in their organization's values**, not because the values are wrong, but because they don't see them live out consistently in decisions, systems, and leadership behavior. The real work of culture design begins when we translate ideals into habits.

Building an Implementation Plan

Culture change rarely fails because of intent. It fails because of execution. Without a roadmap, people default to business as usual. That's why the first step in implementation is to **create a clear, time-bound plan**.

An effective culture implementation plan includes:

- **Specific milestones:** Define what success looks like at 30, 90, and 180 days, then one year.

- **Ownership:** Assign leaders who are accountable for each lever of culture (e.g., People/HR for processes, Communications for storytelling, Business Leaders for modeling).

- **Resources:** Dedicate time, budget, and training support. Culture work can't be a side hustle.

- **Measurement:** Define how progress will be tracked — surveys, attrition, engagement scores, or business outcomes tied to culture.

Assigning Ownership and Accountability

Here's a mindset shift that's critical: **culture is everyone's job, but accountability must be named.**

- Executives model culture at the highest level and set expectations.

- People leaders reinforce commitments daily in team routines.

- HR or OD ensures processes don't undermine culture.

- Employees themselves hold peers accountable by recognizing alignment and constructively addressing missteps.

When accountability is shared but not assigned, nothing changes. When ownership is clear, momentum builds.

The Employee Voice in Culture: Ownership Creates Impact

I've spent a lot of time defining the role of leaders in Culture by Design. I thought it was time to pay attention to the role of employees. Excluding employees from the design and implementation process of intentional culture is a risky miss for organizations.

When companies talk about culture, it often sounds like something leaders define in a boardroom and then roll out to everyone else. Leadership crafts a purpose statement, vision, and set of values, and employees are told to "live them."

The problem? Culture doesn't work that way. A culture that's only designed at the top can feel forced or disconnected from the real employee experience. For culture to stick, employees need to be more than participants. They need to be co-creators.

Why Employee Involvement Matters

Employees are the ones who actually carry the culture every day. They turn abstract values into real behaviors, interactions, and decisions. When they're invited into the design process, three things happen:

- **Ownership**: People commit to what they help create.

- **Authenticity**: Culture reflects how work really gets done, not just what's written on a poster.

- **Adoption**: Change rolls out faster because employees see themselves in it.

When to Engage Employees

Timing matters just as much as the method. Here are some moments when involving employees is especially valuable:

- During growth: As new people join, current employees can help through storytelling and interpreting how culture commitments translate into every day actions

- When values feel stale: If culture statements no longer resonate, employees can breathe life into them with fresh language and examples.

- During transformation: Whether it's a merger, digital shift, or new strategy, employees can help translate big changes into daily ways of working.

- Ongoing, not just once: Culture isn't a one-time project. Keeping feedback loops open ensures it grows alongside the organization.

Different Ways to Involve Employees

Getting employees involved doesn't have to mean starting from scratch. Here are a few levels of involvement to consider:

- **Input and Feedback:** Gathering perspectives through surveys, focus groups, and listening sessions ensures values and commitments align with what employees experience.

- **Co-Creation:** Involving employees in drafting values, shaping behaviors, and designing rituals creates a shared sense of authorship.

- **Activation:** Employees play a role in rolling out cultural practices—whether designing recognition programs, contributing to onboarding, or modeling behaviors.

- **Continuous Evolution:** Establishing feedback loops allows employees to surface emerging needs, identify gaps, and suggest adaptations so culture stays dynamic.

Practical Approaches That Work

- **Storytelling**: Invite employees to share stories of when the organization was at its best; these stories reveal authentic cultural strengths.

- **Crowdsourcing Values in Action**: Ask employees to identify everyday actions that best demonstrate the company's stated values.

- **Pilot and Test**: Engage teams in experimenting with new rituals or recognition practices before scaling across the organization.

- **Culture Councils**: Form cross-functional groups of employees who serve as culture advisors, providing insight and helping to activate cultural practices across departments.

The Role of Leaders

Leaders still play an important role; they set direction and define the big picture. But strong leaders know culture isn't something they can hand down. Their job is to create the conditions for employees to contribute and then celebrate the ideas and practices that emerge.

Watch Out for Pitfalls

Employee involvement is powerful, but it can backfire if it's not genuine. A few traps to avoid:

- Asking for input but not acting on it (tokenism).
- Overcomplicating the process with too many workshops and jargon.
- Only involving a select few instead of giving everyone a voice.

Examples in Action

- Southwest Airlines embraced playful in-flight announcements because employees invented them — and they became a signature part of the brand.
- Adobe's "Kickbox" program let any employee test out new ideas, reinforcing a culture of empowerment and innovation.
- One mid-sized manufacturer asked employees to rewrite value statements in their own words. The simplified, employee-driven versions were adopted company-wide and embraced far more quickly than the originals.
- Airbnb gathered employee stories of meaningful experiences, which inspired new rituals like "check-in sessions" to strengthen belonging and purpose.

Communicating the Plan (and the Patience)

Employees need to know the plan exists and that it won't happen overnight. Transparency is essential. Leaders should share:

- Why culture is being redesigned (the *why* gives meaning).

- What the plan looks like (the *what* gives clarity).

- How employees will be part of it (the *how* gives ownership).

- When progress will become visible (the *when* gives patience).

Culture change is a marathon, not a sprint. By setting expectations early, leaders prevent "initiative fatigue" and help employees see this is not another flavor-of-the-month program.

Making Storytelling a Ritual

Stories are one of the most powerful culture tools because they humanize values. One story about an employee living the culture carries more weight than 20 PowerPoint slides.

Organizations that implement well create **storytelling as a ritual**, for example:

- Leaders starting meetings with a "culture moment" story.

- Town halls that spotlight employees embodying commitments.

- Internal newsletters that share short, authentic wins.

- Peer-to-peer forums where employees share how culture shaped a decision or customer outcome.

When stories become a regular rhythm, employees don't just hear the values, they feel them.

Making Culture a Standing Agenda Item

Perhaps the most practical, and most overlooked, implementation tool is the leadership team meeting. When culture is treated as an "add-on," it falls to the bottom of the agenda. When culture is a **standing item**, it signals that it is as important as financials or strategy.

Questions every leadership team should regularly ask include:

- What cultural commitments have we advanced since our last meeting?

- What cultural challenges are we currently facing?

- Are we measuring progress effectively? What does the data tell us?

- How are we modeling culture as leaders in our daily behavior?

By creating this rhythm, leaders normalize culture as a business imperative rather than an HR initiative.

Anchoring Culture in Four Levers

To ensure culture isn't just aspirational, embed it across four levers:

1. **Leadership Modeling** – Employees watch what leaders *do*, not what they *say*.

2. **Processes & Systems** – Recruitment, onboarding, performance management, promotions, and recognition must align with commitments.

3. **Communication & Rituals** – Stories, symbols, and ceremonies make culture tangible.

4. **Accountability & Feedback** – Surveys, feedback loops, and performance evaluations measure culture alignment.

Implementation isn't about perfection; it's about persistence.

Case in Point: Culture in the Agenda

At a health tech services company, the executive team made "Culture & People" the first item on every leadership meeting agenda, before financials. Each leader was expected to share one example of how they or their team lived a cultural commitment that week. Peers discussed each item shared, asked for deeper clarifications of actions taken, and challenged shared examples that were too ambiguous or vague. Over time, this created peer accountability, normalized storytelling, and provided real-time visibility into cultural progress. Within a year, employee engagement scores rose by 15 points, and voluntary turnover in frontline roles dropped significantly. The shift didn't come from a flashy campaign, it came from consistent attention.

Reflection Questions

- Do we have a clear implementation plan with milestones, ownership, and measures?

- How are we communicating the culture journey to employees, so they understand it's a process, not a one-time event?

- In what ways are we giving employees a voice and a role in shaping how culture is lived?

- Where does our culture feel most alive today and how do employees experience that?

- Are we prepared to act on what employees share, not just listen?

- How can we make sure all voices, not just the loudest or most senior, are represented?

- What rituals (storytelling, recognition, symbols) could we implement to keep culture alive in daily work?

- Do our leadership team meetings consistently keep culture on the agenda? How are we holding ourselves accountable for progress?

- Where do our current processes or systems work against the culture we want — and how will we fix them?

Leadership Reminder: Culture change is not a project with an end date. It's an ongoing discipline. Consistency is the differentiator.

Implementation Checklist:

Bringing Culture to Life

☑ **Build the Plan**

- Define 30/90/180-day milestones and a 12-month vision.

- Clarify what success *looks like* in behavior, not just words.

- Secure resources (budget, training, comms support).

☑ **Assign Ownership & Accountability**

- Name specific leaders for each cultural lever (leadership modeling, systems, communication, accountability).

- Build culture expectations into leadership performance goals.

- Ensure accountability is distributed but not diluted.

☑ **Communicate Clearly & Honestly**

- Share the *why*, *what*, *how*, and *when* with employees.

- Be transparent that culture change is a process, not an overnight fix.

- Set expectations for visible progress checkpoints.

☑ **Engage Employees**

- Form culture ambassador or peer-led groups.

- Invite employees to co-create rituals, recognition, and new practices.

- Create safe channels for feedback when the culture isn't working.

☑ **Make Storytelling a Ritual**

- Open meetings with a "culture moment."
- Spotlight employees in town halls or newsletters.
- Capture and circulate stories that illustrate commitments in action.

☑ **Embed Culture in Leadership Meetings**

- Make culture a standing agenda item (before financials).
- Ask: What did we accomplish? Where are we stuck? How do we measure progress?
- Hold one another accountable for modeling commitments.

☑ **Align Processes & Systems**

- Audit hiring, onboarding, performance management, promotions, and rewards.
- Ensure systems reinforce culture rather than undermine it.
- Adapt policies and practices to make commitments real.

☑ **Measure & Sustain**

- Track engagement, retention, customer outcomes, and performance tied to culture.
- Share progress publicly to build trust and momentum.
- Refresh rituals and practices regularly to keep culture alive.

Add your own Notes and Ideas here:

15
STEP FIVE: SUSTAINING AND EVOLVING CULTURE

Designing and implementing culture is only the beginning. The true test of any culture initiative is whether it endures over time and adapts as the organization grows, shifts, and faces new challenges. Sustaining culture requires two things: **discipline** and **evolution.** Discipline ensures you don't let fade into slogans on a wall. Evolution ensures your culture stays alive and relevant in a changing business context.

Culture as a Living System

Culture is not static. It is dynamic, constantly shaped by external forces (market shifts, technology, customer expectations) and internal forces (leadership changes, new strategies, talent coming and going). What worked beautifully five years ago may now feel outdated, or even limiting. The healthiest organizations treat culture like a living system: one that must be nurtured, measured, and recalibrated over time.

Research backs this up. Deloitte found that **83% of executives rank culture as critical to business success, yet only 19% believe they have the "right culture" in place.** The gap often comes from treating culture as a one-time project instead of an ongoing discipline. Sustaining means revisiting, reinforcing, and adjusting — not assuming culture will hold itself together once "installed."

Four Practices to Sustain and Evolve Culture

1. Embed Culture into Core Processes
Culture will only endure if it is woven into the way you hire, onboard, promote, reward, and exit employees. Ask:

- Do our hiring practices select for values as much as skills?

- Does onboarding teach not just *what* we do, but *how* we work together?

- Do promotions and rewards align with culture commitments, or just output?

When culture is embedded into these systems, it becomes self-sustaining.

2. Keep Culture on the Leadership Agenda
Leaders must keep culture visible. This means making culture progress a standing agenda item in executive and team meetings. Leaders should be asking:

- What commitments have we lived out this month?

- Where do we see cracks forming?

- How do we know we are making progress?

When leaders talk about culture as naturally as they talk about financials, the organization takes notice.

3. Refresh Rituals and Stories
Rituals and storytelling keep culture alive. But over time, rituals can grow stale or symbolic without meaning. Refresh them. Invite new stories. Retire what no longer resonates. For example, if your team starts every weekly meeting with a "customer win," shift occasionally to a "team collaboration win" to highlight another part of your culture DNA. The key is to keep rituals dynamic so they reflect the current state of your organization.

4. Reassess and Recalibrate
Build in regular "culture check-ups", just like health check-ups. Conduct annual surveys, run focus groups, or gather data through pulse checks. Ask not only whether employees are engaged, but whether they feel the culture commitments are alive in practice. Use this data to identify where your culture needs strengthening or evolving.

The Evolution Mindset

Perhaps the most important piece of sustaining culture is holding it lightly enough to let it evolve. Culture is the heartbeat of your organization, but even a healthy heart adapts to new levels of activity, stress, and demand. Companies that sustain culture over decades are those that balance consistency with flexibility. They hold tightly to their DNA — the core values and commitments that define them — but remain open to evolving practices, rituals, and behaviors that bring those values to life in changing circumstances.

As leaders, this requires humility. It means being willing to admit when something is no longer working, and courage to try new ways of reinforcing culture without abandoning your DNA.

Reflection Questions

- How are we embedding culture into our everyday systems (hiring, onboarding, promotions, rewards)?

- Is culture a standing part of our leadership conversations, or do we only talk about it in moments of crisis?

- Which rituals and stories feel alive and energizing — and which may need refreshing or retiring?

- When was the last time we conducted a "culture check-up"? What did we learn?

- How open are we, as leaders, to evolving our culture practices without losing our DNA?

The Sustaining Toolkit

1. Embed in Systems

Culture is sustained not just by values on a wall, but by the systems employees touch daily. If those systems send contradictory signals, culture erodes. Alignment makes culture tangible.

- **Hiring & Onboarding:** Ask values-based interview questions; use onboarding to immerse new hires in stories, rituals, and modeled behaviors.

- **Payroll & Benefits:** Do pay and benefits show employees they are valued? Are they fair, competitive, and reflective of commitments to well-being and inclusion?

- **Performance Management:** Are systems reinforcing the right behaviors, not just outcomes? Is feedback tied to values and culture commitments?

- **Talent & Decision-Making Data:** Are systems generating insights leaders actually use to make people-first decisions about growth, retention, and engagement?

- **Rewards & Recognition:** Are promotions, bonuses, and awards linked to cultural commitments as much as business metrics?

- **Exit Interviews:** Do you collect and act on culture-specific insights when employees leave?

2. Keep It on the Agenda

If culture isn't regularly discussed, it becomes invisible. Leaders must treat culture as a standing priority, not an afterthought.

- **Leadership Team Meetings:** Make "Culture" a recurring agenda item. Ask: *What progress have we made? What's working? Where are cracks showing up?*

- **Board Updates:** Include culture in quarterly reports alongside financials. Highlight successes, challenges, and risks.

- **Cross-Functional Forums:** Hold regular "culture check-ins" where different teams share how commitments are showing up in their daily work.

- **Leader Storytelling:** Open meetings with short stories of culture in action — wins, lessons, and moments of alignment.

3. Refresh Rituals

Rituals, the small but consistent behaviors that reinforce culture, can fade if left unattended. They need renewal to stay meaningful.

- **Celebrations:** Are you still celebrating the right things? Add new rituals that recognize behaviors aligned with evolving values.

- **Onboarding Rituals:** Ensure new hires are welcomed in ways that reflect who you are now, not just who you were five years ago.

- **Team Traditions:** Encourage micro-rituals at the team level — like recognition circles, learning hours, or Friday reflections.

- **Company-Wide Storytelling:** Make storytelling about "culture moments" a ritual. For example, monthly spotlights on employees living the values.

4. Measure, Revisit & Evolve

Culture is alive. If you aren't measuring it, you can't improve it. If you aren't evolving it, it will drift.

- **Pulse Surveys:** Regularly measure alignment with values, psychological safety, and engagement. Keep them short, but consistent.

- **Culture Metrics:** Track metrics like turnover, promotion equity, and cross-team collaboration as indicators of cultural health.

- **Employee Voice:** Use focus groups or open forums to dig deeper when cracks appear. Listen as much to informal signals as formal data.

- **Revisit the Blueprint:** Periodically pull out your *Culture by Design Blueprint* — the one you authored as a leadership team. Compare it to what you see in practice today. Are cracks showing up again? Do your commitments still align with your current business reality? Treat this as your north star and recalibrate when needed.

- **Benchmark & Adjust:** Revisit your blueprint annually and refresh as your strategy evolves.

✦ Reflection Questions

- Which of your current systems may unintentionally undermine your stated culture?

- How often does culture show up in leadership conversations, and in what depth?

- What rituals are strong today? Which need refreshing to stay relevant?

- When was the last time you revisited your *Culture by Design Blueprint*? Does it still reflect who you are and where you're going?

- What leading indicators could you measure to catch cultural cracks before they widen?

Leadership Call-to-Action

Sustaining culture is not about achieving perfection. It's about practicing vigilance. Culture is never "done"; it's dynamic, alive, and always in motion. Leaders who sustain strong cultures are those who:

- Keep culture visible in decisions and dialogue.

- Stay curious about cracks rather than defensive.

- Treat rituals and systems as living expressions of their values.

- Return again and again to the blueprint they authored, reminding themselves of the commitments they made.

The mandate is clear: sustaining culture requires rhythm, discipline, and courage. Just as a business would never stop tracking revenue or monitoring strategy, culture deserves the same level of leadership attention.

Case Scenarios

1. Mid-Course Correction (18 Months Later)

Scenario: Eighteen months after launching cultural commitments, a services company noticed cracks: cross-regional collaboration faltered, customer complaints rose, and leaders expressed frustration.
Action: The executive team courageously surfaced the issues, adjusted processes and recognition practices, and reinforced behaviors aligned with their values.
Takeaway: Culture is dynamic; the courage to revisit and course-correct is a powerful leadership signal.

✦ Culture Sustained in Action: A Mid-Course Correction

About eighteen months after rolling out a new set of cultural commitments, a fast-growing services company started noticing troubling signs: collaboration across regions was breaking down, customer complaints were inching up, and leaders were quietly expressing frustration that priorities were misaligned.

At first, the executive team hesitated to reopen the conversation. After all, they had invested months into aligning on their commitments and admitting something wasn't working felt like backtracking. But to their credit, they chose courage over comfort.

They called a special leadership retreat to surface the cracks. What they discovered wasn't failure, it was drift. As the business scaled, some of their original assumptions no longer held. The values themselves were still right, but the behaviors and systems tied to them needed an update.

The team made deliberate adjustments: clarifying decision-making roles, refreshing how cross-regional projects were funded, and reinforcing recognition practices. Within months, collaboration began to recover, and employees felt energized by the fact that leaders were willing to admit course corrections were necessary.

The lesson? **Culture is not a "set it and forget it" endeavor.** The courage to revisit, discuss, and adjust, even when it means undoing something you once championed — is one of the strongest signals leaders can send that culture truly matters.

Case Scenarios

2. Front-Line Turnover

Scenario: A manufacturing company saw rising turnover among front-line managers during rapid growth, threatening engagement and operational consistency.
Action: Leadership investigated, clarified decision-making, revamped recognition, strengthened coaching, and created manager forums.
Takeaway: Signals like turnover reveal hidden cultural gaps, addressing them reinforces alignment and retention.

✦ Culture in Motion: Addressing Front-Line Turnover

A mid-sized manufacturing company had seen rapid growth over the previous two years. Revenue was strong, new products were launching, and customer demand was surging. Yet HR began noticing a troubling trend: **turnover among front-line managers was climbing**, far above historical averages.

These managers were the linchpins of daily operations, responsible for translating leadership strategy into actionable work and maintaining team engagement. Their exit surveys revealed a mix of frustrations: unclear decision-making authority, inconsistent recognition, and insufficient support from senior leaders.

Rather than dismiss the turnover as "growing pains," the executive team approached it as a signal from the culture itself. They convened a cross-functional task force including operations leaders, HR, and recently promoted front-line managers to diagnose what was happening.

The findings were illuminating: some cultural commitments weren't translating into practice at the front lines. Recognition programs favored individual high performers rather than teams, and some managers were left navigating challenging situations without guidance or support.

The leadership team took deliberate action:

- Clarified decision-making boundaries and escalation paths.

- Adjusted recognition programs to reward collaborative success, not just individual output.

- Increased mentorship and coaching for front-line managers.

- Established a monthly "manager forum" to surface issues early and share best practices.

Within six months, **turnover among front-line managers dropped to below historical norms**, and engagement scores rose. The leaders' willingness to acknowledge gaps and act decisively reinforced that culture was **an evolving system, not a static statement of intent**.

Lesson Learned: Cultural drift can emerge in unexpected pockets, especially during periods of growth. The most effective leaders treat these signals as opportunities to listen, course-correct, and reinforce the behaviors that sustain a thriving organization.

Case Scenarios

3. Microcultures in a Growing Tech Company

Scenario: A tech company experienced emerging microcultures within product teams that conflicted with the broader culture, creating silos and uneven behaviors.

Action: Leaders identified inconsistent microcultures, engaged teams to co-create alignment, adjusted rewards, and created cross-team forums for collaboration.

Takeaway: Microcultures are natural growth byproducts; attention and corrective action maintain alignment with core values.

✦ Culture in Motion: Microcultures in a Growing Tech Company

A fast-scaling tech company had experienced tremendous growth in headcount and market reach over just a couple of years. The executive team was proud of their culture of innovation, collaboration, and transparency, values that had fueled their early success.

However, as the company grew, **microcultures began to emerge** within specific product teams and regional offices. Some teams became siloed, hoarding information; others developed informal norms that rewarded speed over quality. While each microculture made sense locally, collectively, they **undermined the broader cultural commitments** of collaboration, shared learning, and customer focus.

Leadership noticed the impact: product handoffs were inconsistent, internal frustration was rising, and engagement scores in these teams were slipping. Rather than imposing a top-down solution, the executive team initiated **listening sessions and cross-functional workshops** to understand the root causes.

Key interventions included:

- Identifying and naming the microcultures and the behaviors driving them.

- Engaging team leads to co-create alignment practices that reinforced company-wide values.

- Revising reward and recognition systems to highlight collaboration and transparency, not just individual output.

- Establishing regular cross-team knowledge-sharing sessions to break down silos.

Over time, these actions **reconnected the microcultures to the larger organizational culture**, while still allowing each team the autonomy to innovate. The process reinforced an important principle: culture is dynamic, and microcultures are both natural and signals of where alignment needs attention.

Lesson Learned: Even the most intentional cultures can fragment as organizations scale. The courage to identify inconsistent microcultures, openly discuss them, and take deliberate corrective action is critical for sustaining the health of the broader culture.

Case Scenarios

4. Leading Through Growth Stages

Scenario: A software company transitioned from start-up innovation to operational scaling. Leadership strengths varied across innovation, efficiency, and customer/employee focus.
Action: Leaders acknowledged differences, aligned on shared responsibilities, and acted in complementary ways while safeguarding the company's DNA.
Takeaway: Cohesive leadership across life cycle stages sustains culture and preserves organizational DNA through growth and change.

✦ Culture in Motion: Leading Through Growth Stages

Growing companies naturally move through different life cycle stages: **initiation and growth, operational efficiency, and customer support/employee loyalty**. Each stage demands different leadership skills and approaches. What's consistent is the need for a **cohesive leadership team** that leans into each other's strengths while maintaining the company's core DNA.

At a mid-sized software company, rapid product adoption pushed the business from start-up mode into operational scaling. Early leaders who excelled at innovation and risk-taking struggled with creating repeatable operational processes. Meanwhile, newer leaders with experience in efficiency and customer operations were ready to implement structure but lacked the instinct for rapid iteration.

Rather than allowing these differences to create tension, the executive team intentionally:

- **Acknowledged** the gaps and strengths across leaders.

- **Aligned** on their collective responsibilities and shared commitments to culture.

- **Acted** to balance innovation, operational discipline, and customer-focused practices.

By leaning into one another's strengths, the leadership team successfully navigated the company through multiple growth stages. They implemented scalable processes without sacrificing innovation, strengthened customer and employee loyalty, and ensured that the company's core DNA, collaboration, transparency, and curiosity, remained intact.

Lesson Learned: Culture survives and thrives when the leadership team models cohesive behaviors across growth stages. Different challenges require different leadership strengths, but maintaining alignment around core values ensures the organization's DNA is never lost, even as the business evolves.

16
FINAL THOUGHTS: THE FUTURE BELONGS TO CULTURE ARCHITECTS

If there's one truth that emerges from this book, it's this: **culture is not a byproduct of strategy — it is strategy.** The organizations that thrive, endure, and leave a meaningful impact are those that understand this, intentionally design their culture, and commit to sustaining it over time.

Culture as a Strategic Advantage

Throughout these pages, we've explored the blueprint, the steps, and the mindset shifts required to become a culture architect. We've seen how intentional culture:

- Aligns leaders and employees around shared purpose and values.

- Drives performance, innovation, and customer satisfaction.

- Serves as the backbone through times of growth, change, and disruption.

Research consistently shows the payoff. Companies with strong, aligned cultures experience higher engagement, lower turnover, and better financial performance. But these outcomes don't happen by chance because leaders intentionally *design, implement, and sustain* culture.

The Role of the Culture Architect

A culture architect is not an HR function or a one-time project owner. It is a mindset, a discipline, and a responsibility. It requires:

- **Courage:** to see the truth about your current culture and address cracks.

- **Collaboration:** to partner with the leadership team and co-create the culture blueprint.

- **Commitment:** to act deliberately, embed behaviors, and hold systems accountable.

Why Now

The future of work is complex. Global competition, technological disruption, remote and hybrid teams, and evolving workforce expectations mean culture can no longer be left to chance. Those who succeed will be the organizations where leaders step forward as architects, shaping environments where people thrive, innovation flourishes, and strategy is executed with clarity and purpose.

Your Call to Action

Becoming a culture architect is a journey, not a project. Start by asking yourself and your leadership team:

- What cracks exist in our culture that we are avoiding?

- Where can we take deliberate action to reinforce our DNA?

- How are we engaging employees to co-create and live the culture every day?

Lead with courage. Align with intention. Act with purpose. The companies that do will not only succeed in business, they will create workplaces people are proud to belong to, leaving a legacy that lasts beyond any single strategy or leader.

The future belongs to culture architects. Will you be one of them?

BE A CULTURE ARCHITECT

LEAD WITH COURAGE. ALIGN WITH INTENTION. ACT WITH PURPOSE.

YOUR DAILY MANTRA:

- See the truth of your culture — strengths and cracks.
- Co-create commitments with your leadership team.
- Embed culture in decisions, systems, and behaviors.
- Treat signals of drift as opportunities, not failures.
- Celebrate stories of values in action.
- Reflect constantly: *Are we living the culture we designed? Are our people thriving?*

CULTURE IS ALIVE. THE ORGANIZATIONS THAT THRIVE ARE LED BY ARCHITECTS:

INTENTIONAL, COURAGEOUS, AND RELENTLESS.

THE CULTURE ARCHITECT MANIFESTO

Lead with Courage. Align with Intention. Act with Purpose.

Mindset

- **Acknowledge:** See your culture clearly, the strengths, the cracks, the unspoken norms.

- **Align:** Partner with your leadership team to co-create shared commitments and ownership.

- **Act:** Take deliberate steps to embed culture into daily decisions, behaviors, and systems.

Blueprint in Action

1. **Assess:** Listen, survey, and observe to understand current realities.

2. **Dive Deep:** Map microcultures, friction points, and opportunities for meaningful impact.

3. **Design:** Translate Culture DNA into commitments, rituals, and practices.

4. **Implement:** Assign ownership, engage employees, and make storytelling a daily ritual.

5. **Sustain & Evolve:** Monitor, measure, refresh, and course-correct relentlessly.

Leadership in Practice

- Make culture a standing agenda item, every meeting, every decision.

- Align systems: hiring, onboarding, performance, recognition, and rewards.

- Treat microcultures, turnover, and engagement signals as opportunities for action.

- Celebrate stories of values in action and reinforce behaviors consistently.

- Reflect continuously: Are we living the culture we designed? Are our people thriving?

Remember: Culture is alive. It grows, shifts, and evolves with your leadership.

The future belongs to those who intentionally design it. Be a Culture Architect.

REFLECTION QUESTIONS/CHAPTER BY CHAPTER

THE CASE FOR CULTURE BY DESIGN: CULTURE = STRATEGY'S SILENT PARTNER

Reflection Questions for Leaders:

- When you think about your current organization, what is the "heartbeat" you feel most strongly, and does it align with the values your company claims to hold?

- Where do you see culture showing up most clearly in daily work: in hiring, meetings, decision-making, or somewhere else?

- What recent experience (positive or negative) revealed the "real" culture of your organization?

PREVENTING CULTURE CRACKS BEFORE THEY BREAK

Reflection Questions for Leaders:

- **Where might inconsistencies exist between what I say and what I reward?**
  – Do my recognition practices align with the values I claim to champion?

- **Am I unintentionally tolerating "cracks" in our culture?**
  – Are there behaviors, attitudes, or exceptions I overlook because results seem to justify them?

- **How clearly do employees see the connection between advancement and our stated frameworks?**
  – Would they describe our promotions and development paths as transparent and fair?

- **What signals am I sending about work-life balance?**
  – Do I celebrate outcomes and sustainable practices—or late nights and constant availability?

- **What role am I modeling as a leader in shaping culture?**
  – Am I leaving culture to HR, or am I personally accountable for the behaviors and consistency my team observes?

- **If employees were asked to describe the "unwritten rules" of our organization, what would they say?**
  – Do those unwritten rules reflect the culture we want—or cracks we've ignored?

- **Am I catching the cracks early?**
  – Do I invite feedback regularly enough to see where trust or alignment may be slipping before it spreads?

THE SCIENCE AND SOUL/THE HARD AND THE SOFT OF CULTURE

Reflection Questions for Leaders:

- Does your organization measure culture the same way it measures performance? Why or why not?

- If you had to describe your culture in one word, would it be an emotion or a system? (And what does that tell you?)

- Which side of culture feels stronger in your organization today — the science (systems, processes, metrics) or the soul (values, meaning, belonging)?

THE LEADERSHIP MANDATE

Reflection Questions for Leaders:

- If your employees were asked to describe your leadership team in one sentence, what would they say?
- Do your leaders model a consistent message about culture, or are employees getting mixed signals?
- Where are you, as a leader, unintentionally sending the wrong cultural signals? What would it look like to course-correct?

CULTURE DNA

Reflection Questions for Leaders:

- Why does our organization exist beyond profit?

- What problem in the world would not be solved if we ceased to exist?

- Does our purpose inspire employees and customers—or could it belong to any company?

- Can every employee on your team clearly explain how their work connects to the company's purpose?

- Where are we going in the next 5–10 years?

- What does success look like when we get there?

- Is our vision bold enough to inspire, yet clear enough to guide decisions?

- Am I modeling passion and commitment to this vision in my own actions?

- Which values are truly non-negotiable for us?

- Can we describe what each value looks like in behavior?

- Are we willing to hire, reward, and fire based on these values?

CULTURE COMMITMENTS

Reflection Questions for Leaders

- What promises are we making to employees, explicitly or implicitly?

- Are those promises realistic and sustainable?

- What do we expect from employees in return, and have we been clear about it?

- Have we defined values as specific, observable behaviors that anyone could recognize?

- Do our leaders model and reinforce these commitments daily?

CULTURE IN MOTION

Reflection Questions for Leaders:

- Which rituals consistently reinforce our Culture DNA and Commitments?

- Are our talent processes aligned with the behaviors and values we expect?

- How do we capture and act on feedback about culture experiences?

- Do our leaders visibly model and celebrate the culture daily?

BECOMING A CULTURE ARCHITECT

Reflection Questions for Leaders:

- **Acknowledge:** Where are the cracks in your culture today that you may be hesitant to name out loud? What's one uncomfortable truth you need to face?

- **Align:** How aligned is your executive team on culture? Where do you see mixed messages or competing priorities?

- **Act:** What's one behavior you personally need to change if you want to model the culture you want to see in others?

STEP ONE: ASSESSING THE CURRENT STATE

Reflection Questions for Leaders:

- What tools are we currently using (surveys, interviews, focus groups) to assess our culture? Where are the gaps?

- When was the last time we asked employees about their lived experiences, not just their engagement levels?

- What cracks in our culture do we already suspect exist — and do we have the courage to name them openly?

- What cultural strengths do we most want to preserve and amplify?

STEP TWO: STRATEGIZE/TAKING A DEEPER DIVE

Reflection Questions for Leaders:

- What microcultures exist within our organization, and how do they align — or conflict — with our enterprise culture?

- Where are the biggest points of cultural friction, and how do they affect performance or employee experience?

- Have we clearly articulated *why* culture matters to our business success right now?

- Are we prepared to have uncomfortable conversations about the deeper truths our culture assessment reveals?

- As an executive, do you see your primary team as your functional area (Finance, HR, Sales, etc.) or as the collective leadership team?

- Where might our executive team unintentionally be sending mixed cultural messages to the organization?

- What would it look like if we truly operated as a Unified Leadership Team? What behaviors would need to change?

- How are we holding ourselves accountable to shared commitments — not just individual or departmental goals?

- If someone outside the executive team were observing our interactions, what culture would they see us modeling?

STEP THREE: DESIGNING WITH EXECUTIVE AUTHORSHIP

Reflection & Practice: Becoming Culture Authors

This chapter has shown why executives must become authors of culture—owning the DNA, defining commitments, and putting culture in motion. The following prompts and exercises are designed for executive teams to use together. They help surface alignment, expose gaps, and create the courage to commit.

1. Reflect on Authorship

- Can you personally state your organization's purpose, vision, and values without looking at a document?

- When employees think of your culture, do they hear your voice, or HR's voice?

- Have you ever made a decision that contradicted the stated values? How did you handle it?

Exercise: In pairs, take five minutes each to articulate your organization's purpose, vision, and values in your own words. Compare notes. Where do you align? Where do your words differ? What does that difference reveal?

2. Translate Values into Commitments

- Choose one of your values. Ask: "What do we promise employees around this value?"

- Then ask: "What do we expect in return?"

- Finally, ask: "What behaviors must be non-negotiable if this value is real here?"

Exercise: As a team, create a chart with three columns:

5. Value

6. Our Promise to Employees

7. Our Expectation in Return

8. Non-Negotiable Behaviors

Fill it out for each value. Then ask yourselves: Are we willing to live this, even when it costs us?

3. Spot the Cracks

- Where do your current processes or rituals look "strong on paper" but crack under the weight of unclear values or weak commitments?

- Which commitments feel authentic and doable, and which feel hollow or aspirational?

Exercise: Review one current talent process (e.g., performance reviews, promotions, recognition). Identify:

- How is it aligned with values and commitments?

- Where does it contradict or ignore them?

- What one change would make it reinforce your authored culture?

---

4. Culture in Motion Audit

- What are your existing rituals (big or small)? Do they reinforce or dilute your culture?

- Which talent processes currently reward or punish alignment with values?

- Where do you invite ongoing feedback about culture, and how often do employees see you act on it?

Exercise: With your team, create a list of three rituals, three processes, and three feedback loops in your company. For each, rate them on a scale of 1–5:

- 1 = undermines our culture

- 3 = neutral, no real impact

- 5 = reinforces our culture powerfully

Commit to redesigning at least one "1" into a "5."

---

5. The Courage Check

- Which commitment is hardest for you, personally, to live consistently?

- If the culture you are authoring demands it, are you willing to change—or would you rather step aside?

Exercise: Silent reflection: write down one behavior you know you must model better for your commitments to be real. Then share it with the team. Invite the team to hold you accountable.

STEP FOUR: IMPLEMENTING CULTURE BY DESIGN

Reflection Questions for Leaders:

- Do we have a clear implementation plan with milestones, ownership, and measures?

- How are we communicating the culture journey to employees, so they understand it's a process, not a one-time event?

- In what ways are we giving employees a voice and a role in shaping how culture is lived?

- What rituals (storytelling, recognition, symbols) could we implement to keep culture alive in daily work?

- Do our leadership team meetings consistently keep culture on the agenda? How are we holding ourselves accountable for progress?

- Where do our current processes or systems work against the culture we want — and how will we fix them?

STEP FIVE: SUSTAINING AND EVOLVING CULTURE

Reflection Questions for Leaders:

- How are we embedding culture into our everyday systems (hiring, onboarding, promotions, rewards)?

- Is culture a standing part of our leadership conversations, or do we only talk about it in moments of crisis?

- Which rituals and stories feel alive and energizing — and which may need refreshing or retiring?

- When was the last time we conducted a "culture check-up"? What did we learn?

- How open are we, as leaders, to evolving our culture practices without losing our DNA?

- Which of your current systems may unintentionally undermine your stated culture?

- How often does culture show up in leadership conversations, and in what depth?

- What rituals are strong today? Which need refreshing to stay relevant?

- When was the last time you revisited your *Culture by Design Blueprint*? Does it still reflect who you are and where you're going?

- What leading indicators could you measure to catch cultural cracks before they widen?

REFERENCES

BOOKS

- Bridges, W., & Bridges, S. (2016). *Managing transitions: Making the most of change* (4th ed.). Da Capo Lifelong Books.
- Brynjolfsson, E., & McAfee, A. (2014). *The second machine age: Work, progress, and prosperity in a time of brilliant technologies*. W. W. Norton & Company.
- Cameron, K. S., & Quinn, R. E. (2011). *Diagnosing and changing organizational culture: Based on the competing values framework* (3rd ed.). Jossey-Bass.
- Collins, J. (2001). *Good to great: Why some companies make the leap… and others don't.* HarperCollins.
- Collins, J., & Porras, J. I. (1994). *Built to last: Successful habits of visionary companies.* HarperCollins.
- Coyle, D. (2018). *The culture code: The secrets of highly successful groups.* Bantam Books.
- Denison, D. R. (1990). *Corporate culture and organizational effectiveness*. Wiley.Drucker, P. F. (1974). *Management: Tasks, responsibilities, practices.* Harper & Row.
- Edmondson, A. C. (2018). *The fearless organization: Creating psychological safety in the workplace for learning, innovation, and growth.* Wiley.
- Hannum, M. (2019). *Purposeful leadership.* FranklinCovey.
- Kotter, J. P. (1996). *Leading change.* Harvard Business School Press.
- Kotter, J. P., & Heskett, J. L. (1992). *Corporate culture and performance*. Free Press.
- Kouzes, J. M., & Posner, B. Z. (2017). *The leadership challenge: How to make extraordinary things happen in organizations* (6th ed.). Wiley.
- Laloux, F. (2014). *Reinventing organizations: A guide to creating organizations inspired by the next stage of human consciousness.* Nelson Parker.
- Lencioni, P. (2002). *The five dysfunctions of a team: A leadership fable.* Jossey-Bass.

- Lencioni, P. (2012). *The advantage: Why organizational health trumps everything else in business.* Jossey-Bass.
- Pink, D. H. (2009). *Drive: The surprising truth about what motivates us.* Riverhead Books.
- Schein, E. H. (2017). *Organizational culture and leadership* (5th ed.). Wiley.
- Sinek, S. (2009). *Start with why: How great leaders inspire everyone to take action.* Portfolio.
- Sinek, S. (2014). *Leaders eat last: Why some teams pull together and others don't.* Portfolio.

REPORTS & ARTICLES

- Deloitte. (2020). *Global human capital trends: The social enterprise at work.* Deloitte Insights. https://www2.deloitte.com
- Gallup. (2020). *State of the American workplace report.* Gallup Press. https://www.gallup.com
- McKinsey & Company. (2021). *Organizational health: A fast track to performance improvement.* McKinsey & Company. https://www.mckinsey.com
- Society for Human Resource Management. (2022). *SHRM workplace culture report.* SHRM. https://www.shrm.org
- Rosso, B. D., Dekas, K. H., & Wrzesniewski, A. (2010). On the meaning of work: A theoretical integration and review. Research in Organizational Behavior

www.ingramcontent.com/pod-product-compliance
Lightning Source LLC
Chambersburg PA
CBHW040928210326
41597CB00030B/5216